REALIZING
the promise of
Performance
Management

Robert W. Rogers

Published by DDI Press

© Development Dimensions International, Inc., MMIV. Revised MMV.

Published by DDI Press, c/o Development Dimensions International, World Headquarters—Pittsburgh, 1225 Washington Pike, Bridgeville, Pennsylvania 15017-2838.

Manufactured in the United States of America.

Library of Congress Cataloging in Publications Data

Rogers, R.W.

Realizing the promise of performance management/Robert W. Rogers

1. Business   2. Performance Management

ISBN   0-9761514-1-3

10	9	8	7	6	5	4	3	2

Dedication

To the love of my life (since the ninth grade)—my wife and partner, Jan.

To the pride of our lives—our three grown children: Wendy, Jennifer, and Rob.

And to the joy of our lives—our three grandchildren: Shelby, Shawn, and Seth.

RWR

Contents

Part III: The Power of Realization

Preface

Performance management: What an enigma!

A precious few organizations today claim to use it to such great effect that they consider it a substantial competitive advantage. In fact, they won't discuss their process publicly for fear of losing their edge.

For other organizations—and we are talking about a much larger number now—performance management consumes enormous pockets of valuable time and resources, yet yields little satisfaction for anyone involved. For the vast majority of managers and associates, it remains a difficult, boring, occasionally painful, and usually unrewarding task to be wedged onto work plates that are already heaping full.

And yet, performance management is also a process that virtually no major organization can seem to do without.

So which is it—competitive advantage, painful waste of time, or indispensable business process? How can intelligent people be discussing the same subject in such different terms?

The fact of the matter is, they are all correct.

Performance management can lead to a distinct competitive advantage. It can help organizations change rapidly, drive toward a single set of strategic objectives, achieve a desired culture, develop associates, increase retention, and a lot more.

But that's not what is happening in most organizations today. Poorly designed systems are implemented haphazardly, supported inadequately by line management, administered inconsistently, disconnected from other organizational systems, and doomed to generate data no one ever uses. It's little wonder that these systems fail to deliver anything remotely close to a competitive advantage.

It's also no surprise, then, that so many managers and even more associates are not feeling the love for the performance management process. Why should they?

This book is about realizing the promise of performance management. "How is that supposed to happen?" you might ask. The answer does not lie in your organization becoming a corporate boot camp, nor implementing a new, therapeutic communication practice. The answer is not software (although that can help), nor is it a better form (although poorly designed forms can work against users). Ironically, the answer to this question is "By applying common sense."

So, who should read this book? *Realizing the Promise of Performance Management* was written for line managers—particularly senior line managers—and especially those who are dissatisfied with their current performance management process as a tool to execute business strategies and get results. It also was written for human resource professionals who want to provide their organization with something more than a process that no one likes and that has very little impact. And if HR wants to be a more strategic player with their senior line managers, this is the book for them.

Caution: This book is not about the "how-to" of performance management. Instead, it is about the "whys": Why spend time doing it right? Why insist that senior executives model the process? Why track how well the system works? And most of all, why demand that managers become skilled users of the system?

What can an effective performance management system do for your organization? The answer, as the case studies in this book will show you, is *get results*. Not only will your organization realize the bottom-line results that executives want, but it also will become a more focused company that retains the best talent, outperforms its competitors, and sustains those outcomes over time. With all that's to be gained, can you afford not to read this book?

Prologue: The Nightmare

A well-known food company found itself in the right business at the right time, as adult consumers were looking for healthy alternatives to the fast-food avalanche engulfing their children each day. But, while the timing was right, the company's growth rate was not—at least in comparison to its competition. It was growing by only 2 to 4 percent per year, compared with 12 to 14 percent for its competitors.

The company was very traditional and hierarchical, and while it provided decent revenue returns, its parent organization wanted more. To get this arm of the company growing again, the parent organization brought in a new president—who was seen as very aggressive and entrepreneurial—from another division. After a few weeks at the helm, he began to understand the scope of the challenge facing him.

Indeed, that challenge was daunting: The senior team lacked a clear sense of direction, priorities were muddled, passion for the business seemed to have evaporated with the latest new product flop, and each senior executive had a different view of what was needed to fix the problem.

And this malaise had seeped down from the top—associates frequently misunderstood the strategic direction and lacked clear accountabilities. They couldn't see how they contributed to the organization's success. Their energy sagged, and emulating their leaders, their passion for the business faded.

The senior leaders' inability to agree on priorities proved to be a prime reason for the flagging associate morale and their sense of lost direction. In fact, the executives couldn't have been more divided on their vision for the direction of the company. The VP of Research and Development lobbied for the quick launch of another new product to erase the bitter taste of the failed new product. The VP of Marketing, who believed the company wasn't very good at developing new products, wanted to pursue new applications for its existing, successful offerings. The Head of Manufacturing pushed for opening a new manufacturing facility in the Northwest, where distribution was very sparse; but, the VP of Sales pressed for a third-party distribution system to supply the Northwest, which would postpone the cost of a new manufacturing site until sales increased enough to justify the expense. Meanwhile, the CFO looked to cut costs throughout the company to improve margins.

Amid this high-level chaos, performance appraisals were carried out only sporadically across the functional units and for the chief purpose of determining merit pay increases. But even then, some units didn't use appraisals consistently. Performance management was seen as a human resource system that was primarily administrative and not very helpful.

PART I

Why You Should Care About Performance Management

CHAPTER 1

THE PROMISE AND THE FAILURES

Here's the promise of performance management: Those organizations that: 1) create clear accountabilities linked to their key business drivers, 2) communicate effectively and involve their associates in managing their own performance, and 3) focus as much time on developing people as they do on evaluating them will be the companies that forge a competitive advantage through this most powerful system.

It's as simple as that. Need proof? In these pages you'll read about how Elisabeth Fleuriot (president of Kellogg France) improved her organization's bottom-line results. Or how Paul Rutledge (CEO of HCA MidAmerica Division) reduced turnover by 60 percent and saved $6 million a year while boosting associate job satisfaction. Or, look to British Telecommunications' BT Exact, where CEO Stewart Davies raised the performance bar in the research division by driving clearer expectations at all levels and by championing his organization's performance management system.

In his book, *Execution: The Discipline of Getting Things Done* (2002), Larry Bossidy focused on driving the implementation of a business strategy through direct and clear accountabilities. Consider what has made a Jack Welch, a Michael Dell, or a James Kilts so effective, and you'll find their focus on this same issue. They have all used performance management as a tool to lock in the focus on their organization's key priorities, and they have all been very effective. Each of these leaders has created a competitive advantage for his company through this process.

My 30-plus years of experience in working with hundreds of organizations all over the world have only strengthened my deeply held belief that there is a right way and a wrong way to use a performance management system. My great frustration continues to be that more companies do not take advantage of this tool.

Some leaders have never experienced the benefits of a smoothly operating, effective system and consequently don't really understand what can be gained. Others don't commit to the rigor and discipline needed to maximize the benefits and desired results. This is simply flabbergasting— once a senior leader gets it, he or she will never retreat! Just ask them—we have, and their response is all too familiar: "I'd never manage any other way. I wouldn't know how to drive business results without it!" You cannot create a high-performance culture without a strong performance management system in place; yet, many senior executives demand high performance without the rigor and discipline needed to power it.

But progress is being made and more research is being conducted to prove this point. Table 1.1, first published in a Harvard Business School study conducted by John Kotter and James Heskett, summarizes the impact of a performance-enhancing culture on organizational performance. It shows some phenomenal results in critical variables that most company leaders would die for.

Table 1.1: Impact of a Performance-Enhancing Culture on Organizational Performance

	Organizations With a Performance-Enhancing Culture	Organizations Without a Performance-Enhancing Culture
Revenue Growth	682%	165%
Stock Price Growth	901%	74%
Net Income Growth	756%	1%

The results of this 11-year Kotter and Heskett study were published in their book *Corporate Culture and Performance* (1992). While their work highlights numerous areas that contribute to a high-performance culture, just about every one of them links to the components of an effective performance management system.

My experience in this field over the last 30 years tells me that an organization cannot have a high-performance culture without an effective performance management system. More recent research by Watson Wyatt Worldwide, Hewitt Associates, and our company, Development Dimensions International (DDI), has born this out. For years we have questioned whether cause and effect can be attributed to a performance management system simply because there are so many independent variables in the equation. But whenever we found excellent results or dramatic improvements over time, we also found an effective performance management system in place, driven by senior line management.

Performance Management Versus Performance Appraisal

Notice that I continually refer to *performance management*—and not performance appraisal—as "the system." Many think of performance appraisal as the system, but there is a vast difference between the two. Performance appraisal is a one-time, year-end event during which a manager evaluates a direct report's performance; performance management, on the other hand, is an ongoing process during a business cycle in which the manager and associate are equally involved in:

- Creating a performance plan for the associate.
- Holding frequent, informal discussions to monitor and track performance.
- Coaching to help the associate achieve or exceed performance expectations.
- Having periodic summary discussions in which the associate's performance is compared to expectations.
- Discussing future-oriented developmental activities for the associate.

Table 1.2 highlights the many differences between performance appraisal and performance management.

Table 1.2: Comparing Performance Appraisal with Performance Management

Component	Performance Appraisal	Performance Management
Purpose	To evaluate an associate's performance.	Multifaceted: • To drive performance. • To develop talent. • To set up people for success. • To drive retention/increase job satisfaction. • To drive the culture.
Process	Once a year.	Continuous during a business cycle, with periodic summary reviews.
Associate involvement	Little, if any.	High levels, including: • Input into goals and objectives. • Tracking of own performance. • Frequent check-ins and coaching opportunities. • Input into performance reviews and evaluation. • Developmental planning.
Link to organizational strategies (both business and culture)	Little, if any. On the results side only.	Clear line of sight to strategic priorities and organizational values and culture.
Link to compensation	Mixed—sometimes direct, sometimes not apparent at all.	Linked as one component of an effective compensation system.
Career and/or developmental planning	Little, if any connection.	A major component—developmental objectives and planning are major parts of the system in all cases.
Communications	Typically top-down on goals.	Goes both ways, with major inputs from associates, higher levels of trust, and better identification of process/systems issues.
Impact on job satisfaction	Low. Associates generally hate the process.	High. If done correctly, associates feel engaged with a sense of ownership of their particular performance plan and developmental opportunities.
Correlation with organizational results	None.	Recent research shows very positive correlation.

By definition, performance management is an ongoing process—not a one-time event. The scars left by years of performance appraisals remain in many organizations, as disillusioned appraisees mistakenly attribute their negative experiences to "performance management." However, the organizations that understand the difference and employ leaders who demonstrate the appropriate use of the system have reaped the rewards. Figure 1.1 shows the results of a DDI study (Bernthal, Rogers, & Smith, 2003) on the perspectives of managers who had implemented a more effective performance management system. It shows the before- and aftereffect of an improved system on numerous organizational factors—and the improvements are dramatic.

Figure 1.1: Impact of Effective Performance Management

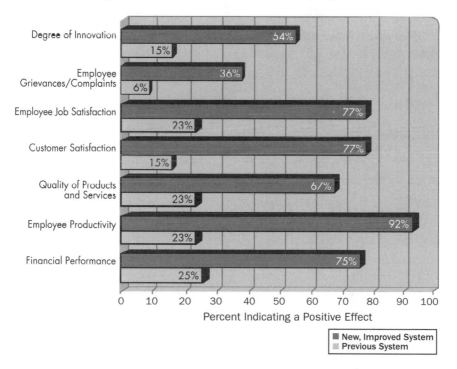

What were the differences? For the DDI clients the previous system was little more than an annual appraisal that focused on relatively tangential items, such as the form, or on the compensation decisions that needed to be made based on the appraisal. There was little involvement of associates in managing their own performance. Our work involved converting an annual appraisal into on ongoing process that used many of the best practices that will be covered in Chapter 6.

The Corporate Leadership Council recently published a study (2002) on what truly makes a difference and what doesn't when managing performance. Figure 1.2 shows the top nine drivers of improved individual performance. These include fair and accurate feedback, clear understanding of goals and objectives, and frequent and effective communication about performance with the purpose of improving it—not criticizing or even evaluating it.

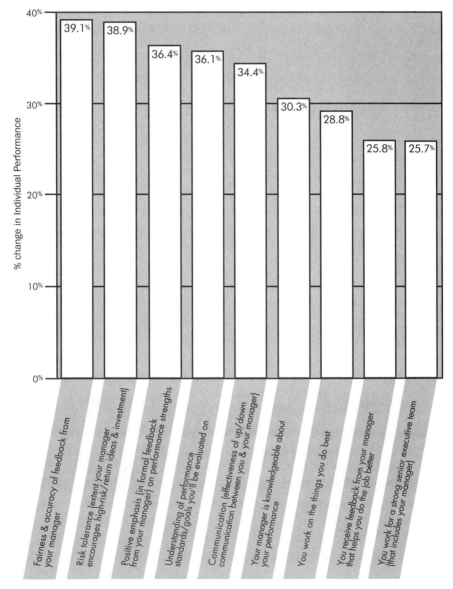

Figure 1.2: Top 9 Drivers of Individual Performance Improvement

So we now know what works. The Council also looked at what doesn't work to improve performance or what was most likely to impede it. Figure 1.3 shows the factors that have the most negative impact on performance. Unfortunately, in many organizations we have seen systems that focus on these negative influences, such as performance or personality weaknesses, rank ordering, or rapidly changing priorities.

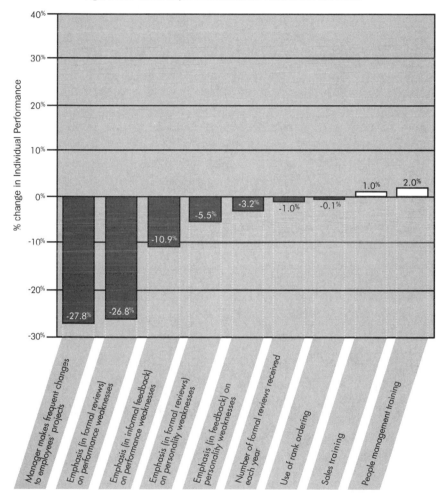

Figure 1.3: What Improves Individual Performance the Least

The Failures

So what makes it so difficult to implement an effective performance management system that powers business results? And are we really seeing much change in leaders' and associates' reactions to performance management systems? The dissatisfaction levels remain very high. A Society for Human Resource Management (SHRM) study (2000) found 53 percent of its respondents were not satisfied with their particular system. DDI's 2003 study (Bernthal, Rogers, & Smith) revealed a similar figure— nearly 50 percent. A recent Arthur Andersen LLP study (Ryan, 2001) found only 27 percent of managers were satisfied or very satisfied with their performance management system; the figure was even worse for their associates (only 17 percent). Clearly, getting the system to work effectively is no easy chore. It takes a concentrated effort by everyone to reap the benefits. Some of the major failures we have seen link directly to the following factors.

1. **Lack of champion/senior management support.**

   This is the primary problem! If senior leaders fail to embrace, use, and reinforce using the system, the chances for success plummet. According to SHRM (2000), in 42 percent of the organizations surveyed, senior management did not review the system at all. Senior management in almost all of these organizations (94 percent) reviewed the system fewer than twice a year. In the organizations surveyed, the managers in only half were held accountable for using the system. How good are we at doing things we aren't held accountable for?

   Now compare that to organizations that have a senior champion, such as GE, Gillette, Dell, Allied-Signal, 3M, Home Depot, Federal Express, or any other company with a strong performance culture. Recently we were in Melbourne, Australia, visiting GE to discuss coaching skills for their managers. The executive we were meeting with explained that she had only one hour to talk because within a few hours her CEO would be starting his online compliance review of GE's performance management system, and she hadn't yet finished documenting all the reviews for her people. She quickly pointed out that very little could damage a senior manager's career at GE as much as the new CEO discovering that the manager hadn't fulfilled his or her requirements under the performance management system.

2. **Failure to tie performance expectations to operating results.**

   According to the SHRM data (2000), 25 percent of organizations **did not** tie their executives' performance goals to operating results. Further, 64 percent of exempt and 83 percent of nonexempt associates' performance goals were not tied to operating results. A FranklinCovey survey (Evans & de la Cruz-North, 2002), which drew more than 11,000 respondents, revealed that only 9 percent believed their work linked to organizational goals (see Table 6.3 in Chapter 6 for more results of this survey). You might wonder how that can be—what would the goals be linked to if not the organization's desired performance results? Unfortunately, our experience confirms the SHRM findings.

Associates need to know how they are contributing and adding value. Senior executives need to focus on those factors that drive results—the greater the focus (that is, accountabilities on the right things), the more likely they will get the desired results. If an organization wants everyone's attention on the top priorities and on focusing on the same results—what better way to do that than by tying each associate's performance goals to the operating results?

3. **No development plans.**

The SHRM study (2000) also reveals that 80 percent of the organizations surveyed had no development or career plans for their associates. DDI's research on retention (Bernthal & Wellins, 2001) shows that the lack of development opportunities is one of the top reasons associates leave an organization (by the way, a poor relationship with the supervisor is number one). If turnover is a concern, why don't more organizations focus on these issues? How can we tell associates that development is important, or—even worse—that people are our most important asset, if we continue to fail to focus on their development? Can we do it without documented plans? Hardly.

4. **No measurement methods to assess system effectiveness.**

Only 2 percent of respondents in the SHRM study (2000) said they evaluate the effectiveness of their performance management system. So how can they improve it if they have no measures of effectiveness? Of those surveyed, 22 percent rated the effectiveness of the system by the percentage of forms completed. How good can this measure be? Quantity of forms completed can't possibly equate to quality of communication, coaching, development, or improvement. How can an organization manage a critical system to drive business results if it fails to measure the system's effectiveness?

5. **No integration of data from the performance management system into other systems.**

The DDI research on performance management (Bernthal, Rogers, & Smith, 2003) shows a direct correlation between organizational performance and how well the performance management system and its outputs have been integrated with other organizational systems (such as selection, promotion, career development, succession management, training, compensation, etc.). However, the SHRM research (2000) points out that only 44 percent of respondents believed their performance management system was integrated with other systems. The disconnect here is obvious (pun intended). How can an organization's systems "talk" to one another—let alone maximize their effectiveness—if they don't share this vital information?

6. **Infrequent communication and lack of associate input.**

The SHRM data (2000) shows that 85 percent of respondents discussed performance evaluations only once a year. That is just not frequent enough. The most effective CEOs (Dell, Welch, Kilts, Bossidy, to name a few) do it quarterly. How does a manager make a midyear correction if he or she doesn't check midyear progress? There is a huge advantage and benefit to more-frequent summary reviews. These don't have to be lengthy, formal conversations. Holding frequent progress checks shows interest, concern, and, most of all, a focus not on evaluating, but on helping associates achieve their performance plan. Conducting frequent discussions about performance also sends the message that the manager cares not only about setting goals, but also about the associate's progress toward meeting them. It's a very powerful message that can have only positive results. So why do so many companies have only one review a year?

7. **Insufficient training for leaders in how to coach and provide feedback.**

A Mercer Management Consulting study (Holsinger & O'Neill, 2002) of more than 300 companies revealed that only 26 percent of associates say their manager provides them with timely and helpful feedback. On average, 50 percent of the executives, managers, and supervisors in the organizations surveyed by SHRM (2000) were not trained in how to provide feedback, and only 33 percent were trained in coaching skills. This statistic alone helps explain why so many leaders and employees are dissatisfied with their organization's performance management system. Giving objective feedback is a necessary component of an effective system; yet, it is one facet that most managers have the least skill and confidence in doing. Wouldn't it make sense to provide training to beef up their competence and confidence? The same applies to coaching. Although most leaders feel they can coach, coaching—like giving straightforward feedback—isn't a natural skill. To many leaders, coaching is merely telling a direct report what to do, based on the leader's own experience. But that is precisely what they should not do! How can an organization not provide training to improve its leaders' coaching skills when developing people is so critical to winning the war for talent? (Remember, one of the reasons people cite most frequently for leaving an organization is that they don't feel they are being developed.)

8. **Too frequent changes to the system.**

   Given the promise of performance management combined with the dissatisfaction that the vast majority of organizations have for their systems, it isn't surprising that 40 percent of the surveyed organizations intend to make significant changes within the next two years. According to the DDI research (Bernthal, Rogers, & Smith, 2003), only 38 percent were confident that they would leave their system unchanged. Our experience in helping organizations has been that the problem is hardly ever the system; rather, it's executing the process and giving leaders the skills to implement the system effectively. Organizations, such as many of those cited in this book, have had the same system in place for years once they have implemented it correctly. Some of our long-term clients have had the same system in place for more than 15 years.

Senior Commitment—a Must

As you can see from these eight problem areas, getting it right takes considerable effort and commitment not only from the people in human resources, but also from senior executives. If the commitment from senior executives is there, the performance management system can be the tool that propels success in almost any direction the organization wants to go. We have seen it:

- Drive customer-retention strategies in the automotive and banking industries.
- Propel a major process improvement to get new drugs to market in the pharmaceutical industry.
- Reduce turnover in the health care industry.
- Support lean manufacturing and six sigma initiatives in many industries.
- Power more efficient processes and increased job satisfaction in federal, state, and local governments.

So there is no question that it can be done. However, the issue always comes back to this question: Why should line managers put their time and energy into making the system fulfill its promise?

The remainder of this book is devoted to answering that important question.

CHAPTER 2

BUSINESS STRATEGIES, PERFORMANCE MANAGEMENT, AND RESULTS

Chapter Overview

In the 1999 *Fortune* article, "Why CEOs Fail" (Charan & Colvin), the biggest lesson in business, and for senior executives in particular, goes something like this: "It isn't strategy *development* that is the most prevalent killer of business results, it is strategy *execution*!" Every senior executive needs tools to execute strategy. Few, if any, tools are more finely crafted to this end than a well-implemented performance management system.

There is an element of irony here. If you are not currently using your performance management system as a power tool for strategy execution, then you are doing worse than simply wasting your organization's time and money. Why? Because a poorly used performance management system not only consumes vast quantities of time and resources, but it also leads participants to perceive it as just another instance of their organization *wasting* their time and resources.

Throughout this book we talk about *realization*. Realization ranges far beyond simple compliance. It's the reaping of the benefit—the culmination of what you set out to do in the first place. The situation is analogous to owning a dairy cow. If you don't use the milk, it's just a lot of work for nothing. You might as well learn how to use performance management now and start getting the benefits sooner rather than later.

This chapter describes the relationship between business strategy execution and a well-implemented performance management system.

What Is "Business Strategy"?

A business strategy is a plan that guides an organization's decisions about its markets, the types of products and services it offers, its relationship with customers, and the distribution channels used to reach those customers. A business strategy emerges from an organization's vision. It's a plan by which the vision is made real. Business strategy development, however, is not explored in this book. Strategy *execution* is!

Strategy Development Versus Strategy Execution

Execution of business strategy is about translating plans into results. It's the business of executives to execute, which isn't always easy. That's why they get the big bucks. But just because executives are at the helm of a given company does not guarantee that they are successfully carrying out their business strategy. All kinds of things can happen. Consider these potential pitfalls:

- Maybe the strategy wasn't communicated in such a way that associates understand it. Or maybe the communication reached some corners of the organization and not others.

- Perhaps the progress toward the strategy wasn't made measurable; you can't manage what you can't measure. Translating a strategy into executable goals requires skill. We all know of organizations that get wrapped up in measuring the wrong things. It's also important to appreciate the difference between lead and lag measures and to know which to use in a given effort.

- It might be that no one is being held accountable for a strategic priority. What, exactly, are you and each of your direct reports responsible for doing? Have strategies been cascaded down to business unit goals? Does everyone in a business unit know what they are responsible for accomplishing and by when?

- Sometimes people are held accountable for getting something done, but they don't have the skills to do what's expected of them. How long does it take to diagnose that problem? Are you providing skills assessment and training to ensure that objectives can be reached?

- Perhaps the right person is not in the right place. What are your mission-critical positions, and are those people ready for what they need to be doing?

- Sometimes a strategy requires a new way of getting work done. New processes and systems are needed.

The Importance of Alignment

So, what is the secret to execution? Success is directly proportionate to the degree of organizational alignment an organization can generate. If you can get the total commitment of all the associates in your organization to a given objective, that objective is as good as achieved. But the more associates you have, the more geographically or functionally dispersed the workforce, and the more unaccustomed they are to rapid change, the harder it will be to attain that alignment. And that's where a performance management system really proves its value. A well-implemented, smartly used performance management system can help translate business strategy into well-articulated, congruent priorities and objectives for the entire organization so that you can move forward with a single purpose.

What role does a performance management system play in alignment? Considering what senior executives should be managing to achieve success, the focus needs to be on three major areas:

1. The **enterprise direction/goals.** The ideal future state of the organization (some refer to it as the vision). Where is the organization headed and why?

2. The **"whats."** What are the key business strategies and strategic priorities that must be achieved to arrive at the ideal future state?

3. The **"hows."** What are the cultural strategies that align with the whats to support the achievement of the strategic priorities? Typically, cultural strategies—the hows—are defined by a set of values or principles (such as customer service, continuous improvement, innovation, bias for action, etc.) that guide associates' behavior.

The performance management system takes these three key facets of the organization and, through defining the accountabilities and measurement methods for each, assigns objectives, competencies, and behaviors for each associate—from the CEO on down to the mail clerk. Figure 2.1 illustrates the role that performance management plays in helping to make that happen.

Figure 2.1: Strategic Architecture

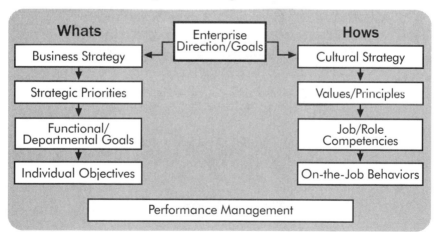

Although we will examine this process further in Chapter 6 (Performance Management Best Practices), Figure 2.1 shows that a performance management system is the key tool in driving an organization's strategy execution. Too often, we see organizations develop comprehensive business plans and strategies, yet fail to channel their associates' energies and passions into the direction defined by those plans.

We know of a worldwide pharmaceutical company that spent $6 million rolling out a new vision, business plan, leadership development effort, and competency model for leaders, only to be frustrated by the lack of organizational change it achieved. The fly in the ointment was that no one—particularly the senior team—was held accountable for the change. The team didn't define process measurement methods to track the desired change, and everyone presumed that this was just another program that would fail in time. A second attempt that included clearer accountabilities at all levels, specific lead measures for results and behaviors, and the CEO's drive to implement the performance management system produced extraordinary results that made that CEO an ardent champion of the performance management system.

As you will see in every case study in this book (starting with the Kellogg example in this chapter), a senior line executive (a CEO, COO, president, president of a division, etc.) is always there, driving the system into becoming a way of doing business that has increased the company's execution skills exponentially.

Creating Alignment in Your Leadership Team

The alignment you achieve will be only as strong as the alignment that exists at the top of your leadership team. Alignment cannot grow from the bottom up. Senior executives need to ensure that you have clearly stated your organization's strategic priorities to your direct reports. They must help each of their direct reports to consider what significant contributions they can make in achieving each of these major objectives.

Once you've worked with each of your direct reports, you'll need to ask yourself if you have allocated sufficient accountability to achieve the desired outcome. If not, where will that accountability come from? If you have, then you've secured a tight alignment, at least through your leadership team. Are you comfortable with how everyone on your team can recreate this process with their staffs? If not, how can you support them in becoming more skilled in this way? This last question might be the best question anyone asks you this week.

The Process for Executing Strategy

In Chapter 1 we mentioned that, in his book, Larry Bossidy focuses on using accountability systems to drive execution. This might sound easy enough, but in the real world of business, it takes hard work and a well-defined process to make it happen.

In our experience there are six steps to executing strategy consistently:

1. **Clarify business strategies.** Execution depends on understanding. Do your direct reports see your strategies the way you do? Your first step is to clearly articulate, enumerate, prioritize, and communicate the business strategy and strategic priorities, and make sure your leadership team understands and agrees to them. How do you determine which are your strategic priorities? They are the four or five strategies with the highest payoffs that your organization needs to be competitive.

2. **Establish measurement methods.** Remember, you can't manage what you don't measure. Consider how you'll keep score of whether your business unit is achieving the strategic priorities. Identifying lead and lag measures for each strategic priority will help you assess progress. Despite the importance of lead measures being championed in *The Balanced Scorecard* (Kaplan & Norton, 1996) and later books on the subject, too often organizations rely too heavily on lag measures instead. Executives need to drive lead measures to ensure that the lag measures are achieved.

3. **Align accountabilities.** Determine the appropriate owners for each strategic initiative and cascade accountability throughout the organization.

4. **Confirm key competencies.** Confirm the competencies every associate in your organization must demonstrate to ensure success. Competencies are clusters or groupings of job-related behaviors, motivation, or knowledge that affect job success.

5. **Match and maximize people.** Assess players against these must-have competencies, matching key people to critical roles to build the strongest team.

6. **Align key systems.** Many organizational systems, such as compensation, information, promotion, and recognition, can reinforce the wrong results or behaviors. Each major system must be reviewed to ensure its alignment with the organization's strategic priorities.

Wouldn't it be great if you had a system in place that could assist you with all six of these steps? This, of course, is a rhetorical question. Your performance management system is going to help you with all of them.

A Strategy-Execution Tool

Performance management is not a strategy-formulation tool; it is a strategy-execution tool. If we look at the six steps for strategy execution, we can see how performance management can and should relate to each.

Performance management systems can be ideal vehicles for communicating strategic priorities throughout the organization. In the process of performance management meetings between each associate and his or her leader, strategic priorities are shared and discussed. The leader articulates how the priorities relate to the associate, and the associate participates fully in determining how he or she can help the organization realize them.

Further, as each leader (starting with you) negotiates the expectations of performance to those priorities with his or her direct reports, responsibilities cascade through the organization. In the end every associate has individual goals that are linked to the business goals. This leads to tight alignment—perhaps tighter than ever before.

While it's a fine thing to have everyone in the workforce on the same page about the organization's strategic priorities and his or her individual role in advancing in that direction, it is not enough. How does a leader know whether progress is being made—or if enough progress is being made? The answer is simple—it must be measurable to be manageable. So, in an effective performance management system, the organization takes every associate's goals, which are already tied to the strategic priorities, and makes sure that it can measure the person's performance to them.

When progress is measurable, each associate can be held accountable for the results. What does that mean? Shall we fire every associate who doesn't achieve his or her plan? We probably won't. What we want are associates who are clear "owners." As regularly as we can, we need to engage one another about our performance compared to our objectives. As managers, we should work to remove barriers to our direct reports' achieving their objectives, not waiting so long that we're caught by surprise when we find out about them. We'll have time to work out a plan to avoid, break through, or circumvent those barriers. After all, most of these problems don't result from associates' willfully digging in their heels; rather, they stem from process obstacles that must be overcome.

But sustaining results over the long term takes even more. What we really want are *champions*—associates who take up a banner and run with it. You cannot create champions through delegation. Champions are self-selected and can emerge only through their own freedom to participate in the process. Performance management presents an almost unique opportunity to empower the individual.

We also want to ensure that all associates can actually do what they have committed to do. Do they have the skills? Are they getting the job done? How will you know? Performance management meetings provide a good forum for answering these questions.

But wait, there's more! If we structure a formal performance management process around the organization's strategic priorities as they pertain to a given group of associates, and if we follow up regularly regarding progress toward those objectives, then we are actively managing toward those strategic priorities. If we listen carefully as we follow up, we will actually hear associates identifying all the process barriers confronting them. How powerful is that!

The following case study illustrates how Kellogg France started from scratch to achieve the alignment we've been talking about.

case study

THE KELLOGG COMPANY, FRANCE

In 2000–2001, sales were flat and profits were declining for the French division of the Kellogg Company. The division's performance was out of step with the aggressive growth goals that Kellogg corporate had set for the next 10 years. By 2004 Kellogg wanted to be in the top quartile of performers in its industry; by 2007 its goal was to become the very best performer.

To hit these ambitious targets, the cereal food giant needed to revitalize its French operation, which serves France, the Benelux countries, Scandinavia, and South Africa. President Elisabeth Fleuriot was determined to see that her French division did its part. She set aggressive goals, crafted a new approach for her organization, and aligned her senior executive team around strategic priorities and core values. Fleuriot's plan was to have Kellogg France become one of the Kellogg Company's top six markets.

The process started with Fleuriot. Working with her senior team, she identified three key priorities—prioritize to win, set the right measures, and execute with excellence—and a core set of values to steer her division in the right direction:

1. We act with integrity and show respect.
2. We are all accountable.
3. We are passionate about our business, our brands, and our food.
4. We have the humility and hunger to learn.
5. We strive for simplicity.
6. We love success.

Starting with her own accountabilities, Fleuriot developed what she called the "Magic Team Road Map"—an action plan with results and behavioral objectives for which she would hold herself accountable. Then she helped each of her senior executives develop an action plan and accountabilities (that is, whats and hows), just as she had done. The team convened the next level of leaders (30 senior leaders) and spent a day developing their road maps and making sure all functional areas were aligned with the division's road map (Fleuriot's plan). They also trained these senior leaders in how to communicate their plans to their staffs and how to align everyone throughout Kellogg France.

For the first time in the division's history, everyone had a performance plan that included objectives aligned with the organization's strategic goals as well as behavioral expectations that linked to its values. In addition, each leader learned to conduct midyear reviews by practicing how to conduct summary reviews, comparing performance to the objectives in the road maps.

As 2002 began, Kellogg France embarked on its journey to improved performance.

Fleuriot also recognized that it would take higher levels of associate job satisfaction and engagement to drive the kind of improved performance she was looking for. She initiated an engagement survey for all associates to gauge how well their leaders were empowering their employees, providing necessary coaching and feedback, and implementing the new performance management process. Kellogg France also conducted focus group meetings to review the pluses and minuses of its new system.

Based on the feedback, the division made adjustments each year to improve this process. For example, in 2003 Kellogg France provided additional training to senior leaders on coaching and feedback. It also provided refresher training on how to set more effective objectives. In 2004 Kellogg France provided additional interpersonal skills training to all managers in the company.

The Results

The results to date clearly reflect the value of Kellogg France's efforts. After two and a half years in the process, the discussion of having accountabilities aligned with division goals has become a way of life. Coaching and feedback have improved considerably, and although the pressure is still there to achieve aggressive objectives, associates rate Kellogg France as one of the best places to work in Europe.

Bottom-line results have improved as well—the flat sales and declining profit trend have been reversed. In 2003 Kellogg France realized 6 percent growth in revenues and a doubling of its profits. The division's market share is rising, and results for 2004 are headed in the same direction. Kellogg France has become one of the top performers in its industry.

Fleuriot attributes much of the division's success to the performance management system (Magic Team Road Map) and the alignment of the senior executives' road maps with the division's goals.

Similarly, McKesson Information Solutions used its performance management system to sharply reduce turnover and significantly improve business results.

case study

McKESSON INFORMATION SOLUTIONS

In 1999 McKesson Corporation acquired HBOC, a publicly held health care IT company. Shortly after the acquisition, the company experienced significant business challenges that resulted in a sharp increase in turnover at all levels of the organization. Employee and customer satisfaction scores also plummeted at the company, now known as McKesson Information Solutions (MIS).

"We faced the departure of the entire senior executive team and a significant number of middle managers," said Terry Geraghty, the former MIS senior vice president of human resources. "Our turnover climbed to 27 percent, and we lost customer confidence. Clearly, we needed decisive leadership action." Further, employee morale was low, and customer satisfaction sagged as the company experienced difficulties in product delivery and quality.

The performance management system was yielding its own surprises: Due to several major acquisitions, there were seven different systems operating in different sections of the division. Some long-time employees had very few appraisals on record, and about half of them had received no review at all.

The newly installed senior management team delivered by immediately establishing goals in four key areas: customer satisfaction, employee satisfaction, accountability, and financial performance. McKesson considered leadership essential to achieving these goals, especially the employee satisfaction component. The challenge? The majority of newly installed leaders had never received formal management training, with many receiving battlefield promotions as a result of the high management turnover. While their technical skills were strong, their leadership skills were missing in action.

McKesson's first step in overcoming the leadership hurdle was building a competency model based on the company's business goals and core principles of Integrity, Customer-Centered, Accountability, Respect, and Excellence.

"We wanted to take these goals and principles and define how they translated into leadership behavior," said Geraghty. McKesson developed a 12-module leadership curriculum called "LEAD the Way" (LEAD being an acronym for Leadership, Excellence, Accountability, and Determination), which ties directly to the identified competencies. Every leader and aspiring leader is required to participate in the certification process, which takes a minimum of two years to complete and is delivered by internal trainers who travel to McKesson locations.

Several programs are integrated into LEAD the Way: a performance management system, a behavior-based interviewing system, and two courses—Results-Based Interactions and Leading Teams—from a multi-day leadership development program.

McKesson launched LEAD the Way in January 2001, putting more than 700 leaders and aspiring leaders through the first module in less than two months. Participants then began moving through the remainder of the curriculum at their own pace and with the flexibility to choose the order they would take the remaining 11 courses. All courses are taught in a traditional classroom setting, but some might be moved online to make them more accessible for employees in remote locations.

In addition to the competency modeling and LEAD the Way program, McKesson addressed its leadership issue through a new succession management program. The company also instituted a revised management incentive pay program tied directly to the balanced scorecard, which factors in customer satisfaction, employee satisfaction, accountability, and financial performance.

The Results

McKesson Information Solutions achieved the following results, due in part to the leadership initiatives launched in 2001:

- The company posted a decline in turnover for 30 consecutive months—from 27 percent to 4 percent.

- Employee satisfaction ratings exceeded norms for high-performance companies.

- MIS employees' satisfaction scores exceeded the norms for global high-performance organizations (2002).

- MIS was named one of *Computerworld*'s 100 Best Places to Work in IT (2003).

- The *Atlanta Business Chronicle* named MIS the second-best company in Atlanta to work for (2003).

- Customer satisfaction rose sharply over time.

- Revenue, operating income, and other financial measures have seen sharp improvements.

- All associates now go through the same performance management process.

- Leaders' effectiveness in implementing LEAD the Way is tied to their pay and bonuses.

This Sounds a Lot Like Management by Objectives

Strategic priorities being clearly stated and rolled down the organization by functional area? Each associate's goals being sourced directly out of the department's goals? Sounds a lot like that dinosaur Management by Objectives (MBO), doesn't it? So, is performance management something new, or is it just another case of an old idea being repackaged and recycled?

What's the difference?

Actually, the differences between the MBO systems of yore and today's performance management are substantial and mostly have to do with the process used.

For starters, performance management is not a case of one-way communication. At each meeting between a manager and direct report—from a president dealing with his senior leaders on down to a sales manager meeting with each member of her sales force— there is a two-way, open-ended conversation. The goals of the individual are not brought into the meeting already written. They are, instead, frequently associate-developed and mutually agreed-upon goals. Not only are objectives set for outputs, but behavioral expectations are set as well.

And there are other differences, but we'll get to those later.

To Get Results, You Must Use the System

Let's be clear: If you design the perfect performance management system and install it exquisitely, you are guaranteed nothing but an exquisitely installed and perfectly designed system—certainly, not results.

You, as a line manager, must champion and use the system.

CHAPTER 3

DRIVING A STRONGER, ALIGNED CULTURAL STRATEGY

Chapter Overview

Corporate or organizational culture is almost as contentious a subject as performance management. Billions of dollars are spent each year trying to forge more-perfect corporate cultures, and for a great many organizations, there is not much to be shown for the investment. Yet, as with performance management, few companies are prepared to abandon the effort.

In short, culture is "the way we do things around here." Not just *some* of us, but the way *all of us* do things. Said another way, organizational culture is the sum of all the behaviors of all the people in an organization. What does your organization stand for? Are you all about customer service? Innovation? Speed? Quality? If the answer to the first question is not obvious (or if you don't like the answer you get), you probably need a strategy to help mold your culture into a more appropriate form.

Formulating cultural strategy is a big job, and just as with business strategy, it is not within the scope of this book. However, it is within the scope of this book to discuss cultural strategy *execution*.

We're not talking about some loosey-goosey, feel-good sensitivity session. Far from it. We're talking about making over your organization in such a way that you get better results because its culture is better aligned with its strategic objectives. If we mention the culture of the U.S. Marine Corps, Starbucks, Singapore Airlines, or Disney, you get a clear mental image. What is the culture in your organization, and does it lend itself to accomplishing its strategic objectives?

This chapter will describe the relationship between cultural strategy execution and a well-implemented performance management system. We'll describe what it looks like when you have realized the benefits of an effective performance management system.

Our last book, *Organizational Change That Works,* began with the following words: "Tomorrow's business success stories will feature organizations that put as much time and effort into their culture strategies as they do their business strategies." We'll stick with that statement. Today, amidst the ruins of numerous failed organizations, those with a clear sense of what they stand for have remained healthy and competitive. We are indebted to the work of John Kotter and James Heskett, authors of *Corporate Culture and Performance* (1992), and Jim Collins, author of *Good to Great: Why Some Companies Make the Leap . . . and Others Don't* (2001), who have documented the impact of corporate culture on financial performance.

What Is "Cultural Strategy"?

A *cultural strategy* is a long-term plan for maximizing the human assets (that is, people) of an organization and living a set of commonly shared beliefs. It defines the type of culture an organization wants to achieve. Will it be customer oriented? Will it be renown for innovation? Will it prize quality above all else?

In the context of such a strategy, the workforce is seen as an asset rather than an expense. A cultural strategy's goal is to make the most of people's contributions by harnessing their convictions, enthusiasm, and passion to support the business strategy.

Typically, an organization's culture is defined by a set of principles or rules. However, although most companies do have a set of values, relatively few manage them into reality. Johnson & Johnson's famous credo stands tall as a notable exception.

For 60 years Johnson & Johnson has used a one-page document to guide the actions and behaviors of its leaders and associates. This credo (reprinted here with permission) has been translated into 36 languages across the world—in Africa, Asia-Pacific, Europe, Latin America, the Middle East, and North America.

THE JOHNSON & JOHNSON CREDO

We believe our first responsibility is to the doctors, nurses and patients, to mothers and fathers and all others who use our products and services. In meeting their needs everything we do must be of high quality. We must constantly strive to reduce our costs in order to maintain reasonable prices. Customers' orders must be serviced promptly and accurately. Our suppliers and distributors must have an opportunity to make a fair profit.

We are responsible to our employees, the men and women who work with us throughout the world. Everyone must be considered as an individual. We must respect their dignity and recognize their merit. They must have a sense of security in their jobs. Compensation must be fair and adequate, and working conditions clean, orderly and safe. We must be mindful of ways to help our employees fulfill their family responsibilities. Employees must feel free to make suggestions and complaints. There must be equal opportunity for employment, development and advancement for those qualified. We must provide competent management, and their actions must be just and ethical.

We are responsible to the communities in which we live and work and to the world community as well. We must be good citizens—support good works and charities and bear our fair share of taxes. We must encourage civic improvements and better health and education. We must maintain in good order the property we are privileged to use, protecting the environment and natural resources.

Our final responsibility is to our stockholders. Business must make a sound profit. We must experiment with new ideas. Research must be carried on, innovative programs developed and mistakes paid for. New equipment must be purchased, new facilities provided and new products launched. Reserves must be created to provide for adverse times. When we operate according to these principles, the stockholders should realize a fair return.

It was this credo that helped Johnson & Johnson's leaders to make the difficult decisions and establish an industry standard for how well a company can react to a product disaster during the Tylenol® tampering events in 1982. And the credo continues to guide them in making key and difficult decisions today. Johnson & Johnson made this set of beliefs a reality.

Executing Cultural Strategy

How do you go about making your values become a reality? There is no magic formula—it requires the same rigor and discipline as it does to drive your business strategy.

Too often, organizations merely pay lip service to their cultural strategy or to the values and principles they claim to hold in high regard. But for an organization that invests the time and effort to carry out its cultural strategy, the rewards can propel that company to previously unattained heights of excellence. Just look at a few of the organizations that have made their culture a priority: Johnson & Johnson, Nordstrom's, Federal Express, and Lexus (Toyota).

Defining the cultural strategy is not necessarily the hard part. Most organizations can easily analyze their markets, customers, and aligned strategies to craft a cultural strategy with an *external* focus, such as quality, customer service, or cost-effectiveness, that affects price. The real challenge is locking in the *internal* focus, which can vary in any direction depending on an organization's history, appeal to prospective employees, style of leadership, structure (hierarchical vs. process orientation), communication systems, and a host of other factors that can affect people's behavior.

There are several key steps to executing a successful cultural strategy:

1. Involve associates in crafting a set of organizational values.

If the senior executive team alone decides what values are important, the chances that these values will take hold in the culture are extremely slim. The involvement of at least a sampling of associates in the value-setting process will help to make the final set of values more people oriented and will better describe the behaviors needed by associates at all levels.

2. Develop an effective communication strategy that makes the business case as to why these values are important.

The communication strategy must start with the CEO or the leader of the organization, and it should spell out exactly why the values are important to the organization's success. All senior executives then must become articulate advocates of the cultural strategy and the criticality of living and modeling the values. To reinforce this importance, first-line supervisors must commit to discussing the values in staff or team meetings and displaying them prominently. And, as leaders make critical decisions, they must be sure those decisions support or reinforce the organization's values; otherwise, the decisions need to be reexamined. The communication strategy must define very specifically what behaviors are expected of everyone.

3. Train all associates in the values.

People need to know how the values translate into behavioral expectations. This requires training. For example, let's say that one of your cultural values is innovation. This, above all other values, is what you stand for (or hope to stand for).

Start by defining the value. You might define innovation as "generating innovative solutions in work situations; trying different and novel ways to deal with work problems and opportunities."

You then might say that innovation is demonstrated by the following actions:

- **Challenges paradigms.** Identifies assumptions in the way problems or situations are defined or presented; sees alternative ways to look at or define problems; is not constrained by the thoughts or approaches of others.

- **Leverages diverse resources.** Draws upon multiple, diverse sources (individuals, disciplines, bodies of knowledge) for ideas and inspiration.

- **Thinks expansively.** Combines ideas in unique ways or makes connections between disparate ideas; explores different lines of thought; views situations from multiple perspectives; brainstorms multiple approaches/solutions.

- **Evaluates multiple solutions.** Examines numerous potential solutions and evaluates each before accepting any.

- **Ensures relevance.** Targets important areas for innovation and develops solutions that address meaningful work issues.

These key behaviors represent the translation of the culture into action. They are all measurable and can be incorporated into the performance management system through individual accountabilities.

Your organization's training function needs to describe how each value and the consequent expectations apply to each associate's position—from senior leaders to mail clerks. In one organization that was driving a culture of customer service and internal partnerships, a CFO proudly announced that he didn't have any internal customers. Other senior leaders and even lower-level associates in the room quickly pointed out to him that while his Finance department wasn't a line function that directly touched the customer, in actuality all the associates that did touch the customer and all those supporting them were his internal customers. Many staff functions in organizations see themselves as controlling—and not service—functions. Such a viewpoint can quickly kill a cultural strategy that attempts to drive collaboration, teamwork, and service.

Similarly, in many instances values can conflict with each other as associates attempt to live more than one at the same time. Training needs to address what the organization wants the associate to do when this occurs (for example, customer responsiveness vs. quality).

4. **Hold leaders as well as associates accountable for living the values.**

Once the cultural strategy has been established and communicated and associates have been trained on the value sets, the next step is to hold leaders and associates accountable for living and demonstrating the values in their everyday lives. This is where the performance management process plays a major role. As in our example of innovation, there are specific behaviors defined for each value that the performance management system can hold associates accountable for as they carry out their roles and positions. Senior leaders need to make sure that associates understand that *how* the job gets done is just as important to the organization's success as *what* gets done. And associates need to realize that senior executives will take action if the associates fail to demonstrate the values. Because we believe an effective performance management system defines both results objectives and behavioral objectives/expectations, this is where accountabilities for living the values are specifically defined.

5. **Measure how well the organization as well as each leader is living the values.**

Just as an organization needs a balanced scorecard or metric dashboard to measure business results, it must have a set of measures that tracks how well associates are living the values. More and more organizations include measures of values into their climate or opinion surveys. Some (albeit relatively few) create a separate survey that focuses solely on the cultural strategy and values and how well the organization and its leaders are living those values.

At DDI, associates complete a Cultural Assessment Realignment and Evaluation (CARE) survey every 18 months to determine how well we are living our six values (driving for client results, reaching higher, engagement, teamwork, quality of life for associates, and integrity). Associates rate the company as a whole as well as their own work team and their leader. This gives us, as senior leaders, a great pulse reading on how we are doing as a company and how well each leader is living and supporting our values.

The CARE survey also identifies the major barriers to our organization's living our values. For example, between our 2000 and 2002 surveys, we noticed a drop in engagement scores in some functional areas.

This resulted in a decision to refresh leaders' skills, with an emphasis on involvement and empowerment techniques. Our turnover rates, which we believed were highly correlated to these lower engagement scores, also had crept above 10 percent for the first time in years. After a significant leadership development initiative that was driven by accountabilities in our performance management system, our scores in the 2004 survey showed marked improvement in the engagement value and associated behaviors. As I write this book, our turnover rate has dropped well below the 10 percent figure as we had hoped.

Once the CARE survey results are communicated to associates at large, all leaders are held accountable for developing a plan to improve the two lowest scores they received for their work area and submitting the plan to me for inclusion in their performance management accountabilities for the upcoming year.

Performance Management and Cultural Strategy

As you can see from the step-by-step process we just described, the performance management system becomes the key driver for the cultural strategy—just as it is for the business strategy. By holding leaders and associates accountable for the behaviors that make the values become a reality, senior executives are communicating how important the cultural strategy is to the organization's success.

There are numerous examples of leaders who succeeded at making their organization's values become reality. Probably the best known is Jack Welch at General Electric. In his 1991 annual report, Welch demonstrated his commitment and support of the prevailing cultural strategy at GE (speed, involvement, and boundarylessness) by describing four types of leaders in GE and what he expected would happen to them as long as he was in charge:

- **Leaders who hit their numbers and lived the GE values.** Welch's reward for them would be promotion.

- **Leaders who failed to hit their numbers, but lived the values.** Welch would give them another chance.

- **Leaders who failed to hit their numbers and live the values.** They would be dismissed.

- **Leaders who hit their numbers but didn't live the values.** Despite getting results, these leaders would be dismissed as well. In Welch's view the long-term effect on the organization would be negative because they didn't model the GE values!

Fred Smith at Federal Express is another senior executive who successfully drove a cultural strategy. That success was based on Smith's belief that leaders need to first take care of their associates, who would, in response, then treat their customers as their leaders had treated them. Smith theorized that, in natural progression, the profits would follow. FedEx's success tells us that Smith's hypothesis was correct. As the organization's senior leader, Smith backed up this belief with action and aligned systems. He initiated a survey that gave associates the opportunity to evaluate company leaders on how well they were living this cultural strategy. Then Smith tied the scores on the survey to leaders' bonuses and further declared that if the leaders' scores did not improve each year, they would not receive a bonus for that year. Ironically, even though FedEx won the Malcolm Baldrige award in 1992, the company's senior leaders did not receive any bonus that year because their leadership survey scores had not improved.

Enron: Corporate Culture Run Amok

Never let it be said that corporate culture is devoid of power that can help an organization climb to lofty heights . . . or perish on its own sword.

While there is no doubt that at Enron some individuals (mainly at the senior level, as we have learned) did many unethical things, there is also no doubt that the organization fostered a culture that actually encouraged them to do so. Enron's systems of oversight, accountability, ethics, and strategic cultural priorities were very seriously flawed.

Enron's corporate culture at the top placed a premium on taking risks, aggressive growth, and entrepreneurship. While these are usually positive values, they were not balanced by attention to corporate integrity, ethics, and the creation of "real" value for clients. The company prospered initially as the culture fostered some values at the expense of others. Senior executives became arrogant in their success, which reinforced the culture and exacerbated the imbalance. As the company grew, the excesses in unethical practices mushroomed. As long as the market remained bullish, Enron thrived. However, when the market began to turn, Enron's stock plummeted and the bubble burst.

Although there were people inside Enron who were aware of the financial shenanigans, there was nothing in place within the organization to support a whistleblower's efforts to call attention to it and, in fact, there was a great deal in place to discourage such action. Again, the culture strongly reinforced a skewed set of values even as the ship began to sink. Because top leadership failed to model integrity, there was little chance to find it in abundance elsewhere in the organization. Employees who wanted to practice more ethical and positive values were stifled in their attempts.

Enron is practically a fable for corporate culture gone wrong: a reliance on short-term stock growth at the expense of real value. In retrospect, this disaster probably could not have been averted, because the company was so culturally bankrupt that it didn't have the moral fiber to right itself.

Enron professed four corporate values: Communication, Responsibility, Integrity, and Excellence. How do you spell "ironic tragedy"?

The Federal Reserve Bank of Kansas City and Cognis serve as stellar examples of how performance management paved the way for major culture change at both organizations.

FEDERAL RESERVE BANK OF KANSAS CITY

The Federal Reserve Bank of Kansas City wanted to create a customer-focused, high-involvement corporate culture. Its objective was to have associates take more direct ownership of their performance and to focus that performance on improving customer service and increasing customer satisfaction.

Top management didn't believe the performance management system in place at the time was structured to drive these critical behaviors, so they instituted a new one. It started at the top with the bank's overall goals and objectives, which were cascaded through each department to ensure goal alignment for all associates. Part of the rollout strategy involved communicating those specific behaviors required for success in a customer-focused environment. The bank was particularly concerned with its ability to compete in the areas of instilling trust, customer service, responsiveness, reliability, and other such measures. Although the bank ranked fairly high on these areas at the time, top management felt it needed to be even more aggressive in driving these key behaviors across all departments to retain the bank's leadership position in its markets.

Top management also knew that many associates without direct customer contact weren't in a position to see how their work linked to customer satisfaction. The new performance management system changed that; it allowed leadership to highlight in specific objectives those job components that supported customer service.

During the initial rollout of the new system, the bank trained its managers for a full day and provided additional training on the interaction skills required to make the system work. In addition, the bank created refresher courses in topics such as:

- The use of relationship-building behaviors in building trust.
- How to give specific feedback.
- The process steps for handing difficult discussions.

The Results

The customer measures referred to earlier remained very high, with a stronger culture focusing on customer satisfaction. The process of realigning goals from the performance management system to the bank's strategic focus became a regular annual event, starting with the senior executives on down. Although many of the original senior executives who implemented the culture change process have since moved on, the culture remains firmly entrenched. Associates take far more control over their performance plans and responsibilities. After many years of use, the performance management system continues to reinforce its value to the organization and its people.

case study

COGNIS

In November 2001 Henkel, the international branded-products giant, sold its Cognis chemicals division to a consortium of three investment firms. Cognis was on its own with a brand-new identity, sales of $3.2 billion euros, 9,000 employees, and locations in more than 100 countries. It was producing five completely different types of chemicals targeted at completely different markets, and it had a mandate to double its sales in five years.

At the time, Cognis had no consistent performance management system in place. Some segments of the organization were holding on to an old 1970s management-by-objectives approach, with no human side to it at all. The system was applied unevenly with no focus on development. Furthermore, there were major cultural differences across the Cognis world that worked against establishing a consistent system. For example, in Latin America and China few, if any, vestiges of a performance management system even existed.

If Cognis was to double its sales in five years, it needed dramatically better strategy execution.

Under the leadership of Mike Miller, president of Cognis' North America operation, the company launched the Target Outstanding Performance (TOP) initiative in the United States. Miller and his implementation team, which included representatives from Cognis' various regions, established four core strategic goals and identified six corporate improvement projects, and they created clear accountabilities for each. Starting with his senior team, Miller drove the alignment to all leaders within Cognis. He and his team tied this effort to a strong cultural philosophy that had been developed previously at the global level. The philosophy was created to help drive the business identity based on what Cognis called "Cultural Principles," which included:

- A passion for customer success.
- One team—one dream.
- Exceptional performance.
- An empowering and rewarding work environment.
- Change and innovation.
- Personal leadership.

Just as the team did for the strategies and projects, it aligned accountabilities for these six cultural principles, which were translated into competencies for the performance management system and rolled out to all associates in North America.

According to Miller, "One of the things I appreciate most about the system is that it forces bosses to have discussions about executing strategy with their subordinates. I think they frequently avoided these conversations in the past."

Cognis elected to link pay to objectives and competency performance. The organization's management development plan also was tied to competencies, which linked to cultural principles. The company required biannual reviews and audited each step of the process.

The Results

The results have been very impressive:

- Associate receptivity has been very high, in part because now they understand how their jobs fit into the big picture. As one employee said, "This is the first time in 15 years I've seen my boss' goals!"
- Cognis now has a much better talent identification process and developmental orientation. This makes it easier to develop associates (which leads to immediate performance improvement) and helps Cognis promote from within—a welcome change that entails many benefits.
- Best of all, there is much greater consistency in how strategic accountabilities are implemented, leading to greater employee satisfaction with the system.
- The system was so successful that it is being rolled out worldwide.
- The focus on financial performance increased and, in a very poor economic year in the chemical industry (that is, 2002)—when many competitors were seeing shrinking revenues—Cognis showed modest revenue growth in the U.S.

Realizing the Benefits of a Cultural Strategy

Want to effect real cultural change? Make every associate in your organization accountable for achieving measurable objectives that speak directly to the cultural strategy you articulate. Use your performance management system along with both formal and informal communications to take a stand for what you value.

Realizing a cultural strategy is a function of execution. Enron makes a perfect case. Its stated values—printed big as life in all the associate handbooks—were no match for the real values. These real values were perhaps best articulated by the slogan inscribed on a paperweight on the CFO's desk: "When Enron says it will rip your face off, we'll rip your face off." Culture and the values that drive it emanate from the top. If it isn't clear what your organization stands for, look in the mirror. The senior leadership team is the source of your culture. Your organization will reflect their actions. How well does *your* performance management system hold leaders accountable for exhibiting those behaviors that are aligned with your stated cultural strategy?

CHAPTER 4

MANAGING AND RETAINING TALENT

Chapter Overview

As I write this book, the economy is improving, and we are seeing the renewed volleys of a war for talent. The origin of this analogy was a year-long study conducted by McKinsey & Co. (Chambers, Foulon, Handfield-Jones, Hankin, & Michaels, 1998) involving 77 companies and almost 6,000 managers and executives. According to this study, the most important corporate resource over the next 20 years will be talent: smart, sophisticated businesspeople who are technologically literate, globally astute, and operationally agile. And even as the demand for talent rises, the supply will be dwindling. This chapter describes the source of this conflict

Regardless of the extent to which you buy into this argument, there is no arguing with the importance to your organization of developing and retaining top-flight people. Further, there is little argument that development is a key to retention.

Let us agree that even if you are extremely particular in your selection process, there is still a relatively small percentage—say, 10–20 percent—of your workforce that is responsible for the lion's share of your organization's momentum. These people are precious. Your ability to identify and develop them from their earliest days in your organization is important because it gives you the opportunity to make them even more effective and because developing them is precisely how you will be able to retain them.

Your best friend in the war for talent should be your performance management system. Not only can it identify the best people with both objective and subjective measures, but it also can be the vehicle for developing this population.

This chapter will describe how your performance management system can help you emerge as a winner in the war for talent.

Talent Management: Winning the War

It has been argued very persuasively that talent is an organization's most precious resource. Here is the argument: Capital is available today if you have good ideas and a good track record. Strategy can't really be patented; if it works well, others will adopt it. Technology is moving so quickly that even if you have the edge today, there is no guarantee that you'll keep it tomorrow. Talent, however, makes all those things work, and if any of them stops working, talent will right your ship. Talent wins—it is your competitive advantage.

As the current war for talent grinds on, it has become much more difficult for organizations to keep their current associates, let alone find qualified replacements. Your likelihood of winning the war depends on your ability to retain the people you have and to attract a crop of new, highly skilled associates. Talent is your leadership today . . . and your leadership tomorrow. It comes from two sources: You can buy it, or you can develop it. The former is very expensive; the latter requires time and effort.

As the Boomer generation moves into retirement, the cadre of up-and-coming, motivated workers promises to be considerably smaller. So as your need becomes greater, talent will be increasingly scarce. That will make recruiting even more difficult, much more costly, and very risky. Regardless of how carefully you screen, failure rates remain higher than anyone would like to admit (for senior-level managers hired from the outside, in excess of 50 percent according to many studies). To darken the prospects further, your own talent will be eyed enviously and recruited strongly by your competitors. It will be essential that you retain the people you have. How do you do that?

Beyond the qualities that make them so valuable to your organization, these top-tier workers are just like everyone else—they just have more options. If they find the waters inhospitable at your organization, they are more likely and able to swim somewhere else. So, it's important for you to know what they want.

What Do People Want from Work?

If so many people are thinking about leaving their place of employment, it stands to reason that a great many of them are not getting what they want from their jobs. So, what do people want from their work? We thought enough of this question that in 2001 we conducted a major survey to answer it. The summary report, *Retaining Talent: A Benchmarking Study,* was written by Paul Bernthal and Richard Wellins of DDI's HR Benchmark Group. Some of what we found is pertinent to this discussion.

Are People Leaving?

According to the study, one-third of those surveyed expected to leave their jobs within the next year. This is a rather sobering statistic. Neither gender nor organizational level made a significant difference regarding those associates' plans. What did make a difference were their feelings about job satisfaction. The greater the level of satisfaction, the less likely associates were to leave. Additional findings related to contemplating a voluntary change in employment included age (that is, younger associates were more likely to leave) and industry. While it's impossible to completely eliminate turnover, there are preventive measures that organizations can take.

The Cost of Turnover

How much does it cost an organization when a crucial position is left vacant? While no universal equation exists to answer this question for all organizations in all instances, one can calculate revenue per associate. Recent studies, including DDI's retention research, have pegged this number at an average of almost $250,000 per key associate; at the executive level or in the case of a strategic value creator, the figure would be much higher. That figure varies by organization, and certainly not all associates create equal amounts of revenue. Even so, your organization is run by people. They bring in revenue by whatever system you have in place. Their showing up makes a difference—as does their absence.

Nor is replacing associates a negligible expense. The cost of replacing a non-management associate runs about 30 percent of that position's annual salary. Replacing a manager costs about 46 percent of that position's salary. Although it's less expensive to replace a non-management associate, most firms must replace them twice as often, so the annual cost of replacing non-management personnel is actually significantly greater. Turnover costs the average large organization more than $27 million per year. Effective performance management can help make this a more controllable cost.

What Companies Do About It

Given its importance and the cost of turnover, retention would figure to be a top priority for most organizations, right? Wrong. For two-thirds of all respondents to our survey, retention was not a top priority. Almost 50 percent had no formal strategy for addressing retention at all.

Further, in a great many instances, HR's views on why associates leave have little in common with the real reasons they leave. Might this lead to retention strategies that miss the mark? Of course! Read on.

Why People Leave

According to the DDI research, here are the top 8 (of 21) reasons, in ranked order, that associates give for leaving:

1. Quality of relationship with supervisor or manager.

2. Ability to balance work and home life.

3. Amount of meaningful work—the feeling of making a difference.

4. Level of cooperation with coworkers.

5. Level of trust in the workplace.

6. Quality of compensation package.

7. Opportunities for growth and advancement.

8. Clear understanding of work objectives.

Notice where compensation ranks—sixth! In fact, most of the factors that associates rank as most important for their leaving can be controlled by an organization without great impact on its bottom line. It should come as no surprise that one of the most effective tools for working with retention can and should be the performance management system.

What People Want Out of Work

On its own, performance management cannot address *all* the reasons associates give for leaving their jobs. But, as described next, it can address several of them.

The Quality of Leader/Associate Relationships

There can be any number of reasons for a problematic relationship between a leader and a direct report. A performance management system that's poorly implemented or lacking in adequate training can only cause such a relationship to deteriorate further. Consider the motivational impact of:

- A lackluster or negative performance appraisal from a supervisor without participation from the associate.

- Feedback unsubstantiated by objective measures.

- Unrealistic goals or goals unrelated to the organization's strategic plans.

- Goals that do not reflect the associate's abilities or attributes.

- Frequent changes in goals.

- The absence of development plans.

None of these situations are likely to improve any working relationship.

In an ideal situation the relationship between a leader and his or her direct reports should be mutually supportive, and the performance management system should be a formal instrument for strengthening their bond. According to some views, one of management's duties is to provide a suite of services to their internal clients—their associates. The system should reinforce the leader's role as a coach, an active developer of the associate, a facilitator for setting goals that clearly link to the organization's strategic direction, and a partner for resolving process issues. The system also should lead the associate to become a more gifted and skilled performer who contributes more to the success of his or her team.

The Ability to Balance Work and Home Life

Can your performance management system reduce the workload on overtaxed associates? Can it arrange for less travel? Or telecommuting? Probably not. But with an effective performance management system that generates open communication between the leader and the associate, the issues of priorities, workload, and alternatives to getting work done all can be discussed in a nonthreatening, problem-solving way. The other advantage of open communication is that it sharpens leaders' awareness of how much work associates are actually handling. This can help the leader realize one of two things: 1) the associate is carrying too heavy a load and some tasks need to be reassigned, or 2) the associate needs to better allocate his or her time.

When communication is open and unencumbered by work-relationship friction, the leader also can see which associates just can't say "no" to requests from internal customers or work units. In any organization those who create real strategic value do, indeed, have a difficult time saying no. They are so driven (which is why they create so much value for you) to make a significant impact that they tend to overextend themselves. Also, their standards are so high that they become workaholics to a fault.

In an effective performance management system, these issues rise to the surface, and with frequent and quality communication, the leader can do a much better job of monitoring and adjusting the balance of the associate's work and home lives.

The Need for Meaningful Work

An effective performance management system gives associates a much more sharply defined sense of how their particular roles fit in the context of the organization—both on a strategic business level and a cultural level. The key is to create a clear line of sight from the goals and objectives in their performance plans to the organization's strategic and cultural priorities. While this is easier to do with associates who are at relatively higher levels in the organization, it also can be achieved for associates further down in the hierarchy. By communicating effectively and showing how their own goals and objectives link to those of their direct reports, leaders can help people see how their performance plans affect the organization's results at the broadest level. Thus, each associate can see how his or her work is meaningful. It all goes back to what people have told us that they want out of their work—to have an impact, to contribute value, and to make a difference. For most, their work represents more than just a paycheck—adding value has become a prime source of job satisfaction.

Similarly, with the more frequent, consistent communication about their performance in a well-run system, associates are more apt to frequently discuss the part they play in helping the organization achieve its goals and objectives.

The Level of Cooperation Among Coworkers

An effective performance management system can get everyone in the workforce moving in concert toward the same strategic objectives. By clearly communicating the expected behaviors that drive teamwork as part of its cultural strategy, an organization underscores the importance of cooperation while discouraging internal competition and turf issues. My personal experiences in the U.S. Air Force and at DDI have reinforced my belief that we can get all associates in an organization to realize that the competition—and not their team members or people in the next department—is the enemy.

An effective performance management system's clear, specific account-abilities of behaviors aligned with collaboration, teamwork, and internal partnerships can transform the culture in which associates work. As mentioned earlier, associates entering the workforce in the last 20 years have put more of a premium on their work environment. A culture that reinforces collaboration and cooperation increases the likelihood that its associates will stay there longer and not risk working somewhere else where such values are not emphasized.

Years ago, to drive these behaviors in our company, we required each leader and associate to carry a performance objective that called for them to strengthen their internal partnerships.

We kept this requirement in place for four years. The objective included these behaviors:

- Identifying the two most critical internal partners.
- Measuring that partnership's level of effectiveness.
- Creating a plan to improve the quality of that partnership/teamwork.

By launching this as part of everyone's performance plan along with increasing our communication about the need for better internal teamwork, we quickly created an environment that was much more conducive to collaboration.

The Level of Trust In the Workplace

Trust, particularly between management and associates, should increase as a function of an effective performance management system. Trust starts with communication and involves being honest, caring about people's careers, and providing the support and coaching required to achieve objectives. Leaders build trust as they interact with associates frequently to discuss both performance for their current roles and development for the future. Nothing builds trust as much as knowing your manager truly cares that you are successful now and years down the line.

The Quality of the Compensation Package

If there is a pay-for-performance component to your organization's compensation package, a properly functioning performance management system will serve as an excellent tool for making sure that everyone understands the program (ordinarily, not a guaranteed occurrence) and has a better chance of enjoying the fruits of solid performance. Nothing kills trust and squelches communication more than ambiguity regarding the impact of performance on one's compensation. The compensation plan can't drive the performance management system (the business and cultural strategies should do this), but it should be directly linked to performance (see Chapter 8). If people feel they are being compensated unfairly, the likelihood that they will begin looking elsewhere for another job rises sharply.

Performance Management and the Opportunities for Growth and Advancement

No other organizational system can help individual associates understand the opportunities for growth and advancement as well as the performance management system. In the best systems, career planning and development—especially for identified talent—is a cornerstone. The development and growth opportunities might focus on competencies, knowledge, or experiences needed for the associate to achieve the performance level described in his or her performance plan. Discussions around strengths and development areas in competencies then become a regular aspect of the system.

Understanding Work Objectives

Work objectives are the bedrock of performance management: The purpose of the process is to mutually develop and agree to a set of objectives that, when combined with those of all other associates, results in the execution of the business and cultural strategies. In addition, if the process is working well when the leader and associate discuss performance objectives, then they also will discuss the level of performance the associate needs to meet or even exceed each objective. This ensures that everyone understands how performance will be rated at the end of the cycle.

Realizing an Engaged Workforce

Every senior executive would like to believe that theirs is a fully engaged workforce. The value of having every associate excited about his or her role and vested in the organization's executing its strategic objectives is almost beyond measure. But how do you realize it? You have to:

- Make sure associates know how their jobs are linked to the organization's business objectives.

- Have a culture that has some nobility to its values. People need a culture they can be proud of.

- Give people an opportunity to own the processes they touch every day. Let them be part of setting their goals, make them partners in their plans, give them the skills they need to succeed, and show them the possibilities for their future by helping them with development plans.

- Make it clear that associates matter to you and your management team.

The following case study shows how a major U.S. health care provider was able to leverage a leadership development initiative with a new performance management system to increase associate job satisfaction and, in doing so, drastically reduce a turnover rate that hovered at 30 percent annually.

HCA, INC. (MIDAMERICA DIVISION)

The MidAmerica Division of HCA comprises 15 hospitals and generates $1.2 billion in annual revenue. In 2000 it found itself with a turnover rate of approximately 30 percent.

And turnover wasn't the only problem dogging the health care giant. MidAmerica President Paul Rutledge was looking for a tool to drive his business strategy with very clear accountabilities. And he wanted line management to see retention as a management issue because of its impact on patient quality, labor management and costs, and process efficiency.

In the health care industry, turnover of nursing professionals and other key technical staff is a pervasive problem. Demand is high for qualified people who can fill certain clinical positions; however, because such individuals are in short supply, they are in a position to change jobs frequently as health care facilities compete fiercely for their services.

The fluid nature of this labor force runs counter to the human capital stability that HCA's MidAmerica Division realized it needed in order to optimize patient care and physician satisfaction and to realize favorable bottom-line results.

Upon reviewing data from an employee perception survey, focus groups, and formalized exit interviews, the MidAmerica Division determined that while compensation and benefits packages were factors in people's decisions to stay or leave, most of those who had departed did so because of a poor relationship with their supervisor, who often was a poor fit with, and ill-prepared for, a leadership role.

"We were promoting people for their technical ability and expected them to be effective or to learn on their own, but then firing them for their behaviors," said Donna Yurdin, director of organizational effectiveness for HCA. "We needed to hire individuals who would be a better fit with the various leadership roles, and then develop behaviors that would make people want to come work at our hospitals, and want to stay and be productive."

The research also showed other causes of the high turnover that, again, pointed back to the critical role of supervisors as well as to the need to introduce or alter various organizational systems and functions. These causes included an ineffective performance management system, insufficient professional development opportunities, absence of clear career tracks, poor communication, and a compensation strategy that failed to link pay to performance and contribution.

The MidAmerica Division began tackling the turnover issue by quantifying the problem and formulating a comprehensive strategy for improving retention. This strategy included a set of initiatives, under the umbrella name "STARS," that addressed multiple facets of associate retention.

A development initiative was launched to provide basic knowledge that managers would need to be successful. The core curriculum for this initiative included learning around the legal aspects of HR, finance (for non-financial managers), productivity, and information systems.

A concurrent "preparation" phase of the leadership development initiative provided leaders with important skills that would improve their ability to lead while also orienting them to the systems the organization planned to implement. This training included extensive work on skills associated with performance management, coaching, and communication.

"We quickly learned through looking at our research that the best way to impact turnover was to give our managers and supervisors the knowledge and skills they needed to create work environments that would attract motivated, engaged employees," said Rutledge.

To begin establishing accountabilities, a competency-based performance management process was designed that allowed associates to assume a more proactive role in determining the course of their current jobs and their professional development. This new system represents a dramatic departure from the previous process, which was driven by backward-looking annual review discussions that focused on past behaviors and contributed little to individual development.

Rutledge started with his direct reports to ensure that all hospital CEOs had clear accountabilities that were aligned with his top seven strategic initiatives. MidAmerica also integrated associate ownership of their performance plans into the process so that people would take a more proactive role in determining the course of their jobs and professional development. To this end, MidAmerica managed to effectively link compensation to performance management so that associates would see the results of their superior performance in their paychecks.

The Results

Every associate is in the performance management system, with accountabilities and a plan aligned with the business initiatives. Turnover has been reduced by 60 percent. The reduction in nursing turnover alone has saved more than $6 million.

Other benefits have included a 26.7 percent improvement in cost reductions and a significant increase in employee satisfaction.

Given these results, it's no surprise that Paul Rutledge is sold on the value of performance management. "Performance management is the way we do things here now—it is how we operate. A recent difficult challenge occurred with the loss of a significant revenue stream. Through the performance management process, we focused on reducing operating expenses while developing alternative revenue channels. We were able to successfully roll out the change because we had clear accountabilities for the different tasks to be accomplished, and we met our objectives. I can't imagine ever again not managing and leading without a system like this."

Rutledge has 21 direct reports. He tries to review each person's goals and objectives every quarter. Two reviews a year is the minimum. While this can be difficult to achieve from a scheduling standpoint, he sees the discussions as key to managing the business. "It's not the form, it's the discussions focused on our key objectives that make the process work so well."

"You Are Simply Average"

It's been said that performance management works quite well for the truly talented and for underachievers, but that it does little for the vast majority of the workforce that falls in between. According to this theory, those identified as high flyers thrive on the recognition, lofty expectations, superior development plans, career plans, and other special attention bestowed upon them. Meanwhile, the theory goes, those underachievers in the bottom tier get a wake-up call that it's time to either shape up or ship out. And that is probably what needs to happen.

But what about everybody else? If you ascribe to this way of thinking, are you not telling them, in effect, that they are average? Are they not getting the message, whether you articulate it or not, that despite their efforts, the organization does not recognize them as "talent"? Because most people believe themselves to be better than average, are you not implying that they are falling short? If so, surely your performance management system is no source of motivation for these associates. You'd be better off trashing your system, right?

Not so fast!

Think about it. Where did your people come from? Didn't you select them with considerable discretion? If your selection process was a good one, they never were average—they were picked to be the best possible matches for the work you needed them to do. If that isn't true, then you need to reexamine your selection process. (We won't be doing that in this book.)

The worst you should be able to say about the vast majority of your workforce is that "they are steady, consistent performers." Isn't that what you want?

When we at DDI assist organizations with their performance management systems, we recommend the middle rating, "Meets Expectations." If everyone in the organization was to meet expectations in his or her performance objectives, the CEO would hit the desired revenue numbers and be very happy indeed. Meeting expectations is what better-than-average associates are expected to do! Many organizations—particularly those with systems that tend to inflate evaluations—struggle with this concept. Part of the training needed for managers is how to deal with this sensitive issue.

CHAPTER 5

ENGAGING ASSOCIATES

Chapter Overview

W. Edwards Deming, that guru of quality, believed performance appraisals ran counter to the objectives of an organization. He believed that if management were managing well, the appraisal that needed to be done was not on the associate's performance, but on the performance of the processes by which the organization produced its goods and services. Scholars and business people alike have spent much time trying to rationalize his very worthy arguments with the realities of the workplace. We just don't seem to be able to function without some sort of performance review process. Today, solely on the basis of labor laws in many countries, not having such a system is almost impossible.

But we do not see a conflict with Deming, who advocated constant conversation about the identification and resolution of business processes. In fact, we're advocating those same things.

What is performance management about (that is, as we are discussing it, not as it's currently practiced in most organizations) but an organization's communicating to and engaging its associates around execution of its business and cultural strategies, both on an individual and a companywide basis?

If you were going to spend $2,000 per year per associate on something (typically what organizations invest each year to operate their performance management system), wouldn't you want it to be an intense, personal exploration of strategy execution?

What we're talking about is a significant paradigm shift in what performance management sounds like and, therefore, in what it yields. If each associate is accountable for a number of business strategy-related objectives that he or she has had a role in formulating, when it comes time to account, what will those conversations sound like?

They should sound like either:

- Mutual agreement about acknowledging the success achieved.
- Conversations about what processes went wrong.

If it's the former, everyone walks away happy and recognized; if it's the latter, some serious problem solving needs to occur.

These communications are worth the investment. And we think Deming would agree.

What Was Deming Right About?

Deming believed that performance appraisal, a one-time, year-end evaluation (as opposed to performance management), was a bad idea, and we happen to agree with him. He believed (and quite correctly, in our view) that performance appraisal:

- **Blames the people rather than the faulty business processes they are responsible for running.** This makes sense. The preponderance of research shows that if business processes work well, performance is great. If business processes are faulty and the people employed to staff them are blamed, that will not effect performance improvement. What's needed is a vehicle that excels at funneling upward communication about the faulty business processes, not a vehicle that holds accountable those not in a position to correct the problem. This happens quite frequently.

- **Destroys teamwork.** By evaluating individuals rather than teams, Deming argued, organizations pit one associate against another. The competition becomes more important than the synergy possible within a team. This is true for small work groups as well as divisions. And when performance appraisal is linked to individual rewards and bonuses, Deming claimed that teamwork is even further compromised. Deming would have thought forced distribution systems to be pure heresy.

- **Fosters mediocrity.** By using standards and goals as a basis for performance appraisal—even if they are high standards—an organization is providing a stable signpost around which performance tends to settle. Because it's important that the standards are met (and merit pay will reinforce this importance), associates are less likely to take risks. In the absence of such risk taking, innovation and the possibility of much greater performance and productivity are abandoned.

- **Focuses on short-term goals.** Simply by setting short-term goals (even if longer-term goals are stated), associates tend to concentrate on achieving them—even to the detriment of the organization's long-term interests.

- **Decreases self-esteem, increases fear, and reduces productivity and motivation.** Although appraisals deliver the message that the person being appraised is performing above or below average, that performance might well be the direct result of business processes or conditions not within the person's control. Appraisals that judge associates and rank them as poor performers frequently foster attitudes that are not in the organization's best interest (such as decreased self-esteem, fear, and lack of motivation). In some instances an organization might be rewarding behaviors not because they were particularly productive, but because the business conditions were favorable. In these situations inappropriate behaviors are often reinforced.

What Was Deming Wrong About?

So how can Deming be right about his critique of appraisal and still be wrong about abolishing performance appraisal? Arguments can be made regarding each point. For instance, consider his belief that appraisal destroys teamwork. In performance management (as opposed to performance appraisal), we advocate reaching agreement on objectives by discussing the support that will be needed from key partners in order to achieve them. Likewise, if, as part of the cultural strategy, organizations emphasize teamwork or collaboration, competencies that reflect these values should be part of the behavioral expectations set each year. These techniques can make effective performance management systems drive teamwork and collaboration, not destroy it.

But there is a larger issue. Performance management (again, versus performance appraisal) is a process more about achieving goals, developing competencies, planning a career, and gaining the engagement required to realize all these things than it is about appraisal. Do we think managers need to provide feedback to associates? Yes, we do. But this feedback should occur more often than once a year. Leaders should be coaching associates all year long on their performance toward the goals set in their performance plan. If an associate receives an appraisal that is in any way a surprise, that surprise is a condemnation of the organization's performance management system.

The way to run a performance management system is to have each associate track his or her own performance, based on measures agreed upon in an initial planning meeting. Further, conversations—both formal and informal—should be occurring all year long between the associate and his or her leader about the progress being made. There should be no surprises. And as for ratings, we believe in evaluating performance, not the individual. We advocate a three-level scale: Exceeds Expectations, Meets Expectations, and Below Expectations. And associates should be able to answer the ratings question for themselves. Deming would have supported a performance management system that does this. Performance appraisal systems don't, and that is what Deming criticized.

But wait, there's more! What do we mean by "conversations—both formal and informal—should be occurring all year long between the associate and his or her leader about the progress being made"?

Ongoing Communication

Here is the good news: A point that greatly interested Deming—that organizations should foster communication about work or business processes—is precisely what should be going on all year long in a well-executed performance management system.

We recommend a system that stresses planning and performing over appraisal, one that gets associates seriously involved in planning their performance goals, developing their competencies, and mapping their careers while their manager acts as a coach and reality check. Then, throughout the year associates track their own performance while leaders check in with them formally through regularly scheduled interim meetings and informally by walking around to see how they are doing.

These conversations will do one of two things: They will reveal either that 1) performance to plan is on track or better—in which case, a short celebratory moment might be appropriate—or that 2) some barrier has been encountered—in which case some problem solving would be in order. But it is critical that any problems be identified so that they can be resolved. So many managers and associates dread conversations about performance appraisal, and in organizations in which this is only a once-a-year discussion, who can blame them? But if you can get leaders and associates to communicate on a regular basis about performance to plan, they most often will succeed in meeting expectations. The communication coming out of a performance management system can boost the whole organization's capacity to execute its business strategy.

The Importance of Training in Coaching and Feedback

The ability to expand an entire organization's capacity to carry out its business strategy depends directly on its leaders' communication skills—particularly in giving feedback and coaching. You might recall from Chapter 1 that while most organizations rely on these skills, relatively few are satisfied with their leaders' skill levels or even take the time to train them.

If you want Deming-level communication, then you must have those skills in place.

So, what is a "coach"? A coach is a safe source of performance advice. A coach supports associates in setting challenging goals and then supports them in achieving those goals by providing training, advice, feedback, focus, an occasional kick in the pants, and a more frequent pat on the back. A coach makes sure associates have what they need—in terms of skills and resources—to get the job done.

According to college football coaching legend Lou Holtz, "A coach is someone who makes you do what you would never do yourself, so you can become the person you always wanted to become."

To use an analogy, think of leaders and associates alike as players in a sport. Organizations must ask themselves, "Do we want to play as amateurs or as professionals? Are we playing weekend soccer or on a World Cup level?" If your answer is the latter, coaching is essential.

It takes great coaching to jump-start an organization's executing ability to a world-class level. Coaches who can challenge, inspire, assist, and continually remind associates of their ability to meet their own challenges do not come along by accident. They emerge because a leader has chosen that role and has worked hard to develop the skills to become adept at it.

Organizations develop skilled coaches in direct proportion to the degree to which they value the role. How highly does your organization value a good coach?

An Ongoing Process

Organizations that seek to influence their associates' performance need to stress one simple maxim: Communicate! A large measure of the benefit you'll derive by following the suggestions in this book stems from your performance management system providing both a structured context for discussing performance execution and a momentum to extend those conversations into ongoing, informal dialogs. Here are some guidelines for conducting these discussions:

1. Talk often.

The critical *how* of performance management is, in fact, *when*. The term that's long been in use is *continuous conversation*. Managers should have three or four performance-related conversations with each direct report in the course of a year. A review of progress toward previously defined, measurable goals should be part of each of these discussions. *Don't* accumulate performance issues for one dreaded session at year's end.

Continuous feedback gives the associate an opportunity to adjust behavior as he or she goes along. In this way, performance appraisal is not an event confined to the formal procedure required by an organization. The real work is what comes between.

2. Communicate expectations clearly.

Without communicated expectations, associates fill in the blanks on their own. A large part of the leader's role is communicating expectations and the reasons for them. Knowing what's expected can be particularly important to someone whose role is changing.

3. Provide positive feedback—it's a necessary ingredient.

Industrial psychologists (as well as marriage counselors) say people handle criticism best when it's delivered in a ratio of one criticism to three compliments.

4. Link comments about past performance to future goals.

People can't change the past, but they can influence what they do from this point forward. Therefore, structure your conversations around the constructive action that can be taken in the future. For example, "If you didn't achieve your objective, let's look at why. What can we do to make sure that you can achieve similar objectives for next year? Are there developmental areas we can focus on to help?"

5. Think like a coach.

Start being the coach. Look for *coachable moments*—those occasions that give you, as the leader, an opportunity to create wisdom in the associate. Performance management is about more than conversation —it's about the manager's attitude, his or her stance. Think in terms of relationship and practice performance management as a significant part of your relationships with direct reports. If you don't think your managers are skilled coaches, ask yourself, "What am I going to do about that?"

So What's a Manager For?

Companies achieve results not by managing numbers, but by managing the people who do the things that make the numbers. A leader must get close to his or her employees and communicate more than ever before. There is no other way to translate business goals into desired human behaviors, the core of a leader's job. The following case study provides a good snapshot of the value of communication in an effective performance management system.

GETTING THE BUGS OUT

A client of ours had a problem: Their IT department had some very lofty goals around turnaround times for releasing customized software solutions to their clients. Because it rushed to cut delivery times, many clients were receiving software riddled with bugs and glitches. How buggy was it? The IT department was receiving 130 emergency change orders per quarter—entirely too many!

The department head reported directly to the president who, having come up through sales, was not a technically savvy individual. He knew a problem existed but didn't know how significant it was, what processes or human factors stood in the way of fixing it, how to fix it, or what measures would indicate that healthy progress was being made toward fixing it.

In the context of performance management, this problem became a conversation between the department head—acting as the primary problem-solving resource—and the president—acting as a facilitator. How did the president know he was not being taken advantage of by the IT director? He had learned through the six year history of the existing performance management system how this director went about setting goals, so he could trust the director's proposed measures.

As an outcome of this performance management conversation, a review of the R&D and QA processes occurred. It was revealed that in the pressure to complete projects quickly, the quality assurance process was being circumvented. Skipping the QA process allowed bugs and glitches to slip through to the clients who, in turn, called in their emergency change orders. With the true cause revealed, new objectives were set that required the IT manager to change the process and remedy the issue. All this occurred in the context of a healthy performance management discussion.

Imagine that once per year every associate in your organization, in the context of performance management conversations, identified and solved just one process problem. That would go a long way toward justifying that invisible performance management budgetary line item, wouldn't it?

The following case study shows how one organization realized a dramatic ROI from its rollout of a performance management system. Getting managers' engagement in the process was the key.

case study

SENSIS

Sensis is a leading Australian advertising and information company, managing brands such as White Pages®, Yellow Pages®, CitySearch®, and the iconic Trading Post® classifieds. Approximately three-quarters of the Australian population (age 14 or older) uses at least one of these products every month.[1]

Sensis aims to be the major player in local Australian advertising and search, and its growth strategy includes the development of online, voice, and wireless search solutions tailored for the local market. To meet this objective, Sensis places a high priority on its "people commitment" to personal and career development of its staff.

As part of this commitment, Sensis monitors employee satisfaction with human resource issues through its Employee Opinion Survey and follow-up focus groups. Initially, the survey revealed that "employees have had less than good experiences with the performance management process." Previous initiatives had improved the frequency of performance management activities, but not the quality of the process or interactions. To address this need, University of Sensis—a learning institute established for Sensis employees—initiated a comprehensive training solution that was rolled out to the entire organization's leadership team. The objectives of the performance management training were to:

1. Help drive a high-performance workplace.

2. Better align individual performance with the organization's business priorities and cultural strategy.

3. Develop a more shared responsibility for performance management between management and employees.

4. Give all employees the ability to develop objectives, identify competencies needed for success, create development plans, measure progress, assess performance, and plan for the future.

[1] Source: Roy Morgan Research, October 2003–September 2004.

A comprehensive measurement process allowed Sensis to track reactions to the program and gauge participants' confidence levels in managing their performance before and after the training. Participants rated their ability in 14 critical skill areas, from "not confident" to "highly confident." These areas included linking individual performance objectives to the overall Sensis vision and values, identifying appropriate development opportunities, and tracking their performance.

The University of Sensis wanted to improve the quality—rather than the quantity—of employees' performance management experience. That could happen only if leaders within the organization boosted their skills and confidence in applying them.

The training did the trick—post-training evaluations of a group of 47 leaders revealed that their overall confidence to effectively manage performance grew by an average of 44 percent. They also were 55 percent more confident in their ability to provide balanced, timely, and specific feedback, and 50 percent more confident in their ability to have an honest discussion of performance ratings. In addition, nearly half of leaders indicated they were more confident in tracking and discussing the personal development plans (PDPs) of their staffs throughout the year.

The Results

The results of the survey for each critical skill area are detailed in Table 5.1 below and on the next page.

Table 5.1: Improvements Attributed to Performance Management Training at Sensis

Behavior/Skill	% Improvement
Linking individual goals to the organizational vision and values.	37.74%
Analyzing development needs and discussing a variety of development options with staff members.	42.31%
Determining methods for tracking and monitoring own performance.	36.36%
Sharing the responsibility of making performance plans work between manager and staff member.	46.38%
Determining methods of tracking and monitoring staff member performance.	46.74%
Using STAR/AR to provide balanced, timely, and specific feedback.	55.21%

Table 5.1: Improvements Attributed to Performance Management Training at Sensis (cont'd)

Behavior/Skill	% Improvement
Writing goals that include all elements of the SMART principles.	48.42%
Defining performance management and how to complete the PDP templates at Sensis.	40.57%
Understanding what factors drive job satisfaction.	38.40%
Planning and reviewing the "whats" as well as the "hows."	42.29%
Tracking and discussing PDPs through the entire performance cycle.	49.63%
Using PDPs as a development tool to discuss career planning.	49.64%
Discussing "recommended rating" with staff members based on evidence gathered through tracking.	50.00%
Identifying development opportunities through tracking performance and interim discussions with staff members.	40.07%

Using a technique developed by Schmidt and Hunter (1983, *Journal of Applied Psychology*), Sensis calculated a return on investment (ROI) resulting from its leaders' and employees' increased skills and confidence. The method involved converting improvements in leader skills to a dollar value, based on salary. When leaders or employees improve their skills, their value increases in proportion to their salaries. Using the behavioral change ratings, Sensis estimated the dollar value of the improvements based on salary and then subtracted all of its program costs. The calculations revealed that the ROI to the Sensis business was nearly $2.2 million, or $10.60 per dollar of costs.

Sensis' General Manager of Human Resources George Elsey summed up the impact of the training effort as "a really effective program that not only supports the strategic direction of the company, but also increases the practical skills that leaders and employees can use effectively in the business every day."

PART II

What Does an Effective Performance Management System Look Like?

CHAPTER 6

PERFORMANCE MANAGEMENT BEST PRACTICES

Chapter Overview

Best practices in performance management are clear-cut and well understood. They boil down to a healthy dose of common sense. While none are counterintuitive or obscure, they also are neither commonly applied. In brief, here they are:

1. Align performance management to support business goals and drive results.

2. Cascade accountabilities to all levels.

3. Balance the whats and hows in the process of setting expectations and reviewing performance.

4. Train managers and associates in the skills they need to realize the benefits.

5. Manage the system as a process—not a one-time event.

6. Promote shared ownership.

7. Link performance management to other systems.

8. Evaluate system effectiveness regularly and identify process improvements.

9. Have line management drive the system.

Looking back at Chapter 1, you'll see that the absence of one or more of these best practices can be found at the root of the failures noted on those pages.

We are not particularly interested in why these practices are not put into effect. In our consulting experience we have seen them in place frequently enough to know that there is no magic involved in implementing a solid system. We know that if the system is strong and used correctly, clients realize results that more than make up for the costs associated with running a performance management system.

Best Practices

There are no secrets to the best practices for performance management. In fact, they are surprisingly predictable and logical. Equally surprising is that so many organizations attempt to run performance management systems without one or more of these practices in place.

1. **Align performance management to support business goals and drive results.**

   We've spoken of this practice often thus far, but the point cannot be emphasized too much.

   It seems almost too obvious: Everything your organization does should support achievement of its strategic objectives. Did you ever hear of an organization that focused too much on making its strategic objectives? Performance management is a primary vehicle for doing this. The degree to which you align your performance management system to your business goals is likely to be the degree to which you are successful in driving results.

   Figure 6.1 illustrates this alignment. Your vision and mission lead to the formulation of both the business strategy and cultural strategy. We refer to the business strategy as the whats; these are the things that, if accomplished, will lead your business to fulfilling its mission. We refer to the cultural strategy as the hows. Your culture imbues the organization with the values and behaviors required to accomplish your business objectives. They are how you get results—whether it's through the strength of your commitment to quality, your ability to innovate, your dedication to detail, etc.

Figure 6.1: Driving Accountability

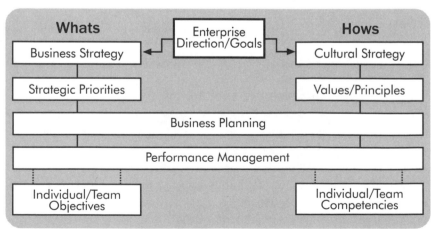

Business strategy dictates strategic priorities—the handful of measurable targets that, if met, enable your organization to achieve its strategy. Similarly, your cultural strategy drives the articulation of your values or principles.

Business planning is a series of conversations, negotiations, and problem-solving exercises during which goals are spelled out and prioritized and accountabilities for achieving the strategic objectives are assigned.

And performance management is the vehicle for rolling out your business plan.

So, why is alignment to the business goals a best practice for performance management? Shouldn't it be the other way around (that is, why isn't alignment a best practice for strategy execution)? Well, It's reflexive. To some degree, you cannot have one without the other. If your performance management system is not closely aligned to support your business goals, no one is going to take it seriously. Why should they? The truth is that, deep down, everyone knows that anything not tied to execution of your strategic priorities really isn't very important. Maybe that's why most performance management systems are not taken very seriously.

2. Cascade accountabilities to all levels.

Alignment between the system and your strategic objectives is not enough. You'll want to cascade accountability throughout the organization. This is important for two reasons:

- As the adage goes, the way to eat an elephant is one bite at a time. If you, personally, could accomplish everything in your organization that needs to get done, you'd be the only associate. The reason you have as many associates as you do, presumably, is to get the work done. Everyone shows up to work for a reason, to do his or her part. Everyone in your organization needs to know how the objectives will be achieved. That means allocating appropriate accountability across the organization for each one of your strategic objectives.

- Everyone in the organization is looking for more than a paycheck. They need to understand how they fit in—what makes their efforts worth their paycheck. By breaking down your strategic objectives so that every associate gets the direct link between his or her efforts and the organization's success, you are validating each person's reasons for showing up. You are helping all your associates to understand their particular value in very real terms.

When we think in terms of accountability, we also think in terms of measurement. To hold someone accountable for an objective, there needs to be a mutual understanding of how it will be measured (for example, dollars in sales, number of claims, score on a customer satisfaction survey).

Measurement is an interesting phenomenon. Most organizations measure their results, like units sold, revenue, return on assets, etc. These are called lag measures. The problem with relying solely on lag measures is that you don't know the results until it's too late. Measures are needed that lead the lag indicators. For instance, an organization can measure its strategy to move into an international market by contacting potential customers in a particular country or geographic region and surveying the interest in the products or services it offers. Such findings are called lead indicators. By using both lead and lag indicators in rolling strategic objectives across the organization, managers get a much clearer view of how they are progressing toward their goals. More and more, we see successful organizations guided by a corporate dashboard of metrics, with heavy emphasis on lead measures.

In the following example, a strategic priority has been assigned to the drug regulatory group of a pharmaceutical company (Table 6.1). Both lead and lag measures make clear how performance will be measured. All that remains is to determine the goal for each measure (for example, "eight months to obtain approval from the FDA"). By managing the lead measures and holding associates accountable for them in the performance management system, this division was able to reduce the time needed to obtain approval.

Table 6.1: Example of Performance Measures for a Worldwide Pharmaceutical Company

Strategic Priority	New products to market; quicker approval from FDA.
Accountability	Drug regulatory group.
Lag Measure	Length of time to be approved.
Lead Measure	• First submission acceptance rate/Need for additional analysis. • Number of requests for additional information or clarifying questions. • Process efficiency of proposal submission.

3. **Balance the *whats* and *hows* in the process of setting expectations and reviewing performance.**

   Many organizations attempt to dictate the whats without considering the hows. This is a major mistake. Consider these examples:

   - If some members of your sales force are making their objectives by competing inappropriately with other sales staff, that will eventually lead to internal friction, conflict, turnover, and a host of other organizational problems.

   - If you deliver a product on schedule, but the quality isn't there, you've met your short-term objectives, but in the long run you might experience returned merchandise, customer complaints, or even a drop in revenue as word of poor quality spreads.

   As you'll recall from Figure 6.1, we recommend a different approach. Setting cultural objectives should go hand in hand with the breakdown of your business strategy objectives. While we stated earlier that we are not going to address how to determine cultural strategy, we did touch on the benefits of such a strategy and on how a performance management system can help you realize those benefits through better execution.

   Why is balancing the whats and the hows a best practice? There are several reasons:

   - You need to achieve both your business objectives and your cultural objectives. *Built to Last* (Collins & Porras, 1994) and *Corporate Culture and Performance* (Kotter & Heskett, 1992) both contain research on how the best-performing companies have a strong culture that supports their business objectives. When the cultural strategy is aligned and accomplished, better results occur.

   - The performance management system lends itself equally well to both kinds of objectives: Both are stated from an organizational context, from the top of the organization down; both require determining development, articulation, prioritization, and communication; and both are ultimately refined in one-on-one, two-way conversations. So, why do it twice?

   - Achievement of the business objectives will be facilitated by achievement of the cultural objectives.

   - This is where development plans will be generated.

4. **Train managers and associates in the skills they need to realize the benefits.**

   If you recall the top nine drivers of individual performance improvement (Figure 1.2 in Chapter 1), you'll remember that many of the drivers relate to the fairness and accuracy of feedback from the leader to the associate and the understanding of what is expected in terms of goals and objectives. Meanwhile, the nine drivers that improve individual performance the least (Figure 1.3, Chapter 1) include too much emphasis on weaknesses in formal and informal feedback sessions. If these are so critical to helping people improve their performance, why do so many organizations provide training only on the whats and not the hows (coaching, providing accurate feedback, etc.) of a performance management system?

During our previously mentioned visit to the GE location in Australia, we had an opportunity to discuss that organization's performance management system. We were surprised to discover that GE Australia—certainly a high-performance culture if there ever was one—didn't train its managers in how to conduct performance discussions or to give feedback and coaching. The one complaint people at this location had about an otherwise very good system focused on the quality of the coaching and feedback. They felt it just wasn't good enough. Why is it that the area that has such a strong impact on results is where organizations decide not to provide sufficient training? If you think about the steps in the process and assume managers aren't naturally gifted in these areas, wouldn't it make sense to train every manager in how to:

1. Set and document effective goals and objectives that are specific, achievable, realistic, measurable, and time bound?

2. Set behavioral expectations that are clear, understandable, and actionable?

3. Conduct a "gaining agreement" discussion on the first two items?

4. Track performance during a business cycle?

5. Provide coaching and feedback?

6. Rate performance in both results and behavioral expectations?

7. Conduct a periodic performance review discussion?

8. Create a personal development plan and plans for his or her associates?

9. Conduct a salary increase discussion?

This might seem like a lot, but you can accomplish all the above in just a few days. Most organizations don't devote the time to training because their leaders are too busy. Besides, they reason, how hard could it be to do these things? The fact is, it can be very hard to do them right. So why not give your leaders the skills they need? Leadership skills such as these do not automatically come with a management position. In fact, most managers' greatest fear is having to give a performance review when they know there will be disagreement or when ratings will affect the individual in some negative way (such as for a salary or promotion).

Organizations that take the time to train their leaders get repaid a thousand times over—every time a fruitful feedback session occurs rather than one that results in damaged trust, poor communication, or reduced commitment from the associate.

5. **Manage the system as a process—not a one-time event.**

While many organizations understand this practice, most others do not. Instead, many organizations see the annual meeting between leader and direct report as the sum total of the program. They might see that they are appraising the past year's performance and providing objectives for the associate to perform against for the coming year. Such a program might provide a high, measurable outcome in paperwork or meetings completed, but it will yield few, if any, desirable outcomes. No amount of preparation for meetings will help. Automation will not help. No amount of training for managers in how to conduct performance appraisal sessions will make a difference.

Performance management is not an event; it's a process. Unless leaders provide ongoing follow-up and coaching and then manage as an extension of these meetings, little can happen. No associate is going to take seriously what is discussed only once a year. Most organizations require formal performance meetings once a year; a few meet twice a year; some, even quarterly. Increasing the frequency of formal communication is commendable, but the realization will come as a function of informal communications.

6. **Promote shared ownership.**

If organizationwide objectives are developed, articulated, and prioritized by the executive team and then communicated down through the organization to the individual level, what do we really mean by shared ownership?

On the surface it would seem to be a one-way street. Management says, "Here, folks, you need to hit these numbers." But that isn't quite what we mean. Yes, numbers are rolled down and, yes, they must be met; however, that doesn't mean the conversation is one-way. The more each associate participates as a full partner in this process, the greater will be the shared ownership and the favorable outcomes.

So what are the actions that lead to this best practice? Here is our list for leaders:

- Share business unit goals and your own objectives.
- Provide open, honest, and frequent coaching.
- Schedule periodic reviews.
- Focus on the future and development.
- Spend less time tracking.
- Ensure objectives are achieved.
- Flex plans as priorities change.
- Improve retention.

And for associates, these actions seem to work best:

- Create your own draft plan.
- Track your own performance.
- Take charge of your own development.
- Seek coaching and feedback.
- Participate in your own evaluation.
- Feel ownership, involvement, and commitment

Methods to Increase Shared Ownership

We have found these actions effective in promoting shared ownership of the performance management system:

- Leader communicates business unit goals to associates.
- Leader encourages associates' input into their own performance plans.
- Each associate develops the first draft of his or her performance plan.
- Associates monitor their own progress toward their plans.
- Associates assess their own performance.

At DDI we have instituted a "Bill of Rights" for associates that underpins our company's performance management system and serves to solidify the feelings of shared ownership. We believe strongly that each associate is entitled to each of these rights.

Here is a generic version of DDI's Bill of Rights regarding performance management:

1. You have the right to know the organization's overall business strategies, plans, and critical business issues as they relate to the key result areas (KRAs), objectives, and competencies in your personal performance plan.

2. You have the right to be involved in establishing the objectives and competencies in your plan.

3. You have the right to use all available data to monitor your own performance.

4. You have the right to receive coaching prior to major activities or events.

5. You have a right to receive feedback following major activities or events.

6. You have the right to periodic reviews that include ratings on both objectives (whats) and competencies (hows).

7. You have the right to disagree with the ratings on your review.

8. You have the right to give your manager—and any vice president in the organization—suggestions regarding how they can better support you in achieving your personal business plan or in the operation of our performance management system.

7. **Link performance management to other systems.**

If implemented correctly, the performance management system will provide a great deal of information that can be plugged into other functions. Not linking performance management to other systems means that those systems will function without relevant, available data. What systems should be linked?

- Promotion
- Selection and On-Boarding
- Succession Planning
- Compensation
- Training
- Total Quality
- Strategic Planning
- Career Planning

Figure 6.2: Linking Performance Management to Other HR Systems

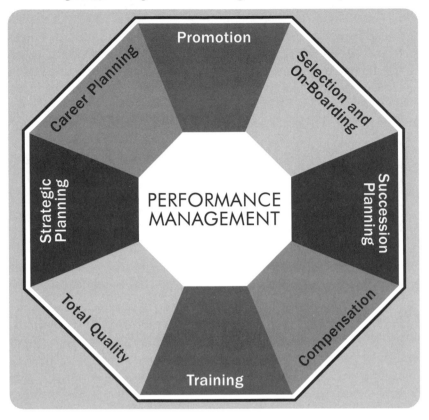

Figure 6.2 shows these links. Some are very obvious, such as the links to compensation (see Chapter 8), training, and promotion; but other links might not be so intuitive (for example, selection and on-boarding). We assume that most organizations today use selection systems that are competency based to fill their open positions. The competencies used to hire individuals into a particular job should be the same competencies that are critical to success in that position. Otherwise, they wouldn't meet the legal defensibility test for job relatedness. And given that they are critical to success, shouldn't these same competencies be evaluated for performance in that job? The answer seems obvious, but in many organizations this is not the practice.

Once hired, an associate should receive feedback on:

• The criteria (competencies) used for selection.

• How he or she was evaluated on each competency.

• How those same competencies are part of the performance expectations in the person's performance plan for the current business cycle.

This doesn't necessarily mean that if 12 competencies were used in the selection system, all 12 would end up in the person's performance plan. However, the competencies deemed most necessary for achieving the key objectives of the position or those needing concentrated development by the person should be reflected in the plan.

The enormous benefit here is that there doesn't have to be a 6-, 8-, 10-, or 12-month wait for a new associate's development focus. It can occur within weeks of employment—just as the person is becoming comfortable with his or her new job and its expectations and goals. This process of providing feedback during selection and linking the hiring competencies to the first performance plan dramatically enhances the associate's on-boarding. We also have found that this process boosts associates to productive levels much more quickly than associates who, after three to four months, still aren't clear about what outputs and behaviors are expected of them. Linking selection and on-boarding to performance management is the impetus to this enhanced productivity.

8. **Evaluate system effectiveness regularly and identify process improvements.**

Amazingly, according to the SHRM study (2000), only about 2 percent of organizations measure the effectiveness of their performance management system. If it's true that we can't manage what we don't measure (and we strongly believe that it is), how could the other 98 percent expect their systems to work well? Given the difficulty of implementing an effective performance management system, periodic measurement of its key components would be an imperative for its success.

But what do you measure? For some organizations the measure is whether managers actually complete the performance review and documentation. But very few organizations measure the qualitative components of the system. A survey we developed for this purpose— and that we have used with some of our clients—measures 10 areas that directly affect the quality of the performance management implementation:

1. Goal alignment.

2. The degree to which goal setting is participatory.

3. Role clarity.

4. The extent to which completion of the performance plan is a shared responsibility.

5. The quality of the feedback.

6. The focus on development.

7. The quality of coaching received.

8. The fairness and accuracy of the review.

9. The value of the review.

10. The completeness of the review.

In addition, the survey asks about the impact of the performance management system on each person's productivity level, overall motivation level at work, quality of his or her relationship with the manager, career development, satisfaction with the job, commitment or loyalty to the organization, and ability to meet work goals. The survey not only provides a clear picture of how well the system is working, but also breaks out the results by department, thereby gauging each leader's effectiveness in implementing the system.

Recently, we had a critical promotion decision to make in selecting a manager to our senior-level operating committee. We had completed our performance management survey, which provided very insightful information on the internal candidates for the position. For the individual we selected, the scores on 7 of the 10 factors we listed previously were higher than for any other manager. It wasn't the only data we used to make the decision, but it did make a difference. We remember thinking, "Given that we are going to give this individual more authority and responsibility with more direct reports, we at least know he will do an excellent job in managing his people through an effective performance management implementation in his new unit."

We have found that the most successful performance management systems usually include some measure to gauge their effectiveness. Seagate (see the case study later in this chapter) is a company that understands the need to measure its system. It measures such items as clarity of goals, the link to Seagate's corporate objectives, timeliness and quality of feedback, openness of communication, and frequency of discussions with managers. Companies such as McKesson, the Federal Reserve Bank of Kansas City, and Merck also use measurement devices to track the effectiveness of these systems.

Without some measurement of the system, organizations fall into the trap of not knowing what needs to be fixed or where. In all our years of working on performance management systems, we have never seen a perfect implementation. There are always areas or departments that need to improve. Once a problem area is identified—either across groups or within one department—additional coaching or training can alleviate the problem. An effective, ongoing evaluation strategy keeps the performance management system alive and dynamic, while avoiding the need for major overhauls every four to five years to work around problems that have exacerbated through neglect over time to become virtually unsolvable.

9. **Have line management drive the system.**

The bottom line of this best practice is "Can we live without it?" Has the system proven so valuable that the organization uses it as a primary means of managing? Effective performance management systems provide extremely valuable information to senior executives on core processes and business trends or patterns as well as on subordinate leaders' skills and effectiveness. Consequently, senior line managers must drive the system by:

- Using it and being a positive model.
- Holding everyone accountable for using it.
- Communicating its importance and value.
- Ensuring the quality of the performance data.
- Acting as an articulate advocate.

If, as a senior line manager, you routinely take all these actions, then your performance management system has become core to your business. If you don't, then you have some work to do in getting more engaged. Here are some tips for increasing your involvement:

- Take ownership of some portion of the process.
- Publish your own performance review.
- Get involved in developing the process.
- Hold yourself and your managers accountable for using the system.
- Regularly communicate with other senior executives and Human Resources on the status or any issues regarding the system.

Criticality of CEO Perceptions and Involvement

Figure 6.3 shows the results of DDI research from a 1997 study (Bernthal, Sumlin, Davis, & Rogers) on the effectiveness of the performance management system correlated with CEOs' perceptions of its value in driving business and cultural strategies. Obviously, if a CEO fails to see the system as a driver of the strategy, the chances of that person's organization having an effective system drop significantly.

Figure 6.3: Relationship Between System Effectiveness and CEO Perceptions

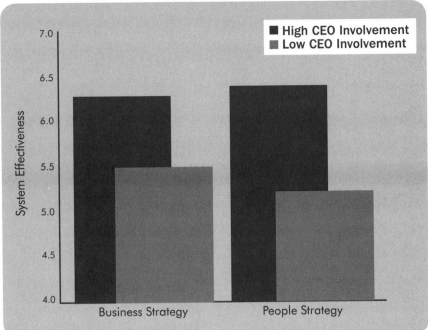

The following case study illustrates how one global, high-tech organization incorporated a number of best practices in reconfiguring its performance management system. In doing so, it was able to eliminate wasted, duplicated effort and direct the focus of its worldwide workforce on executing its stated business and cultural strategies.

case study

SEAGATE TECHNOLOGY

Seagate Technology, a California-based, global high-technology provider of storage technologies (that is, computer hard drives), enhanced the alignment and performance of its global employees by radically reshaping its performance management process.

Seagate's process was in need of an overhaul. In the geographically dispersed organization, employees were often unaware of their managers' goals and lacked an effective process for aligning their efforts to the top business priorities. This resulted in duplicated efforts and wasted resources. Managers and executives in some regions or functions were naturally protective of their own resources and interests, building local silos that created internal competition and conflict. Over time, each major geographic region had created its own performance evaluation processes and systems (many were paper based) using outdated, inconsistent competencies. Employees and management worldwide agreed the process was not adding value and, in many cases, was not being used at all.

At the heart of Seagate's performance management overhaul is an emphasis on "goal alignment" for the 16,000 employees who began using the company's new web-based system. In it, every user has goals that align with his or her manager's goals and that ultimately align with the CEO's goals, which are the company's corporate objectives (best practice 1). Every year the company's senior executives gather for a full-day "Goal Alignment Workshop" during which their individual goals are "scrubbed vigorously" to ensure clarity and alignment at the top of the organization before they are cascaded throughout the company (best practice 2).

Another key component of the new process is a consistent set of Seagate and leader competencies that help to embed the company's values into a personal accountability and also focus the leaders on the five key areas that senior management has determined as most critical for the next three to five years (best practice 3). Each user identifies the competencies he or she most wants to develop and then creates a development plan. That plan is integrated into the performance management online application that helps the person accomplish the goals or grow in responsibility.

The first step in the annual performance evaluation process requires each user to complete a self-evaluation so that employees have ownership and responsibility for their performance during the year (best practice 6). The self-evaluations also provide their managers with feedback to consider during the final performance evaluation. The company also introduced a new rating scale with the new system so that the organization could reset and truly start driving a "performance" culture (best practice 8).

Karen Hanlon, Seagate's vice president of human resources, stressed that effective use of the new performance management process is a key measure in the corporate "people" objective, "To cultivate a diverse, high-performing team environment." In the first year of global implementation, Seagate's Maximizing Alignment and Performance (MAP) initiative exceeded its performance management goals, as Table 6.2 shows.

Table 6.2: Exceeding FY '03 Performance Management Goals at Seagate

MAP (Maximizing Alignment and Performance) Implementation		
FY '03 Measures	FY '03 Targets	FY '03 Actual Results
Goal Setting & Alignment	90% of Indirect Labor Employees have goals in MAP by the end of Q1, with 80% of all goals aligned.	97% of Indirect Labor Employees had goals in MAP by the end of Q1, with 80% of all goals aligned.
Development Planning	90% of Indirect Labor Employees have development plans in MAP by the end of Q2.	93% of Indirect Labor Employees had development plans in MAP by the end of Q2.
Self-Evaluations	75% of Indirect Labor Employees complete FY '03 self-evaluations in MAP.	92% of Indirect Labor Employees completed self-evaluations in MAP by July 9.
Manager Evaluations	90% of Indirect Labor Employees have FY '03 performance evaluations completed in MAP by their managers within the CMC-agreed-upon performance rating distribution guidelines.	100% of Indirect Labor Employees had FY '03 performance evaluations completed in MAP by their managers within the CMC-agreed-upon performance rating distribution guidelines by July 29.

In an employee survey completed toward the end of the first year of its new performance management system, Seagate was able to achieve some impressive results compared to employees at other U.S. companies, who responded to the FranklinCovey xQ™ survey, which polled more than 11,000 U.S. workers in 2002 to measure their "execution quotient." Table 6.3 shows the comparison between the FranklinCovey survey and the results of a survey ("Focus!") conducted by Seagate.

Table 6.3: How Seagate's Execution Results Compare to National Results

FranklinCovey xQ™ Results	Related Seagate "Focus!" Survey Results
44% of U.S. workers surveyed said they clearly understand their organization's most important goals.	84% believe Seagate's leaders have communicated a clear vision of the future.
19% of U.S. workers surveyed have clearly defined work goals.	80% have clear goals or targets to guide their performance.
9% believe that their work has a strong link to their organization's top priorities.	91% clearly understand how their job supports Seagate's corporate objectives.
12% report their individual performance is reviewed monthly with their manager.	71% believe their manager provides timely and helpful feedback.
34% say they work together in a "win-win" atmosphere.	79% believe they work on a high-performing team.
19% say their organization helps them meet its most important goals by removing barriers.	76% say their manager informs them when priorities change to avoid wasting time and effort.

At the end of the first cycle of its new performance management process, Seagate surveyed its top management. MAP received strong support, as shown in Table 6.4, which indicates the percentage of executives who strongly agree or agree with each statement.

Table 6.4: Percentage of Seagate Executives Who
Support the Performance Management Process

Survey Question	Strongly Agree/Agree
MAP has enhanced communication about goals within my organization.	96.3%
MAP has provided for better goal setting in my organization than in prior years.	94.4%
The percentage of people in my organization having development plans has increased over prior years.	92.6%
The feedback process between managers and employees has been enhanced by the use of the MAP application.	92.6%

Seagate's results have not happened by accident. A full year went into preparing top management's goals prior to launching the process to the organization at large. And, a concerted implementation and communication plan was put into effect along with the process changes. Most importantly, clear measures for the success of the new process were established and tracked vigorously during the implementation (best practice 8).

The following case study shows how a recently privatized, former government organization leveraged a performance management system to change the mind-set of its workforce, thereby enabling it to compete successfully in the private sector. The organization used several of the best practices described in this chapter.

QUEENSLAND TREASURY CORPORATION

In the early 1990s, the Queensland, Australia, government decided to privatize the portion of its treasury department that raised government bonds to fund major state infrastructure projects, such as highways, bridges, and schools. Initially, this corporation, called the Queensland Treasury Corporation (QTC), was a small organization (15–20 people), but it quickly grew to more than 150 people, thanks to its amazing success as a private company with an independent board.

However, the transition from a public service company to a more independent entity was not without its trials and tribulations. Challenges included changing the mind-set of associates and, consequently, the aligned behaviors—from a government mentality of monitoring, regulating, and controlling, to a more innovative attitude through which meeting customers' goals and objectives, including business development, became the imperatives. This quantum change included getting associates to understand that their accountabilities for accomplishing their goals and objectives would directly affect their compensation. No longer was the standard government raise of 3 to 4 percent automatic. No longer could a study or research project take months to accomplish.

Soon after the QTC was established, senior leaders realized the magnitude their change efforts required. After developing a strategic business plan, they implemented a performance management system to refocus and redirect associates' energies on "activities that would help create and realize the new business model they had created" (best practice 1). The strategic plan was broken down into clear account-abilities for the senior executives, each team, and each team member (best practice 2). The technical experts (in this case, economists, public accountants, financial analysts, etc.) needed to shift their behaviors from a highly independent, analytical focus to one that combined appropriate risk management, collaboration, and teamwork with the need to achieve bottom-line results (best practice 3). The performance management system implementation included extensive training and feedback on the new behaviors needed (best practice 4) with a revised compensation system linked to performance, which affected up to 20 percent of an associate's compensation (best practice 7).

Initially, the dramatic change seemed overwhelming for some, and the emphasis on performance objectives and goals and the discipline needed to accurately track performance were foreign to some who had worked in government their entire careers. However, with the support of the management team and persistence of the human resources team, the new system eventually took hold and began to steer activities and results in a very positive direction.

Now, more than 10 years later, the organization is still growing and successful. Many factors contributed to this success, but the installation of the performance management system was one of the major initiatives that drove those needed changes. Today, the performance management system is institutionalized into QTC's strategic-planning process and is accepted as the method of driving performance and results in the organization. QTC's written policies reflect it, the leaders support it, and the organization conducts regular audits and reports on the system's effectiveness (best practice 8). Senior leaders report regularly to their independent board on associates' performance ratings, trends in performance, and actions to improve the system. This same support goes to every team leader in the company. No salary reviews are conducted unless the performance review is documented and in the system.

One of the unique applications that added to QTC's success in driving change was how the organization used competencies to drive the desired behavior changes (best practice 3). Because one of the first changes made was structural (going from departmental silos to teams to be able to service their clients in different areas), management realized they needed to place a premium on the nontechnical areas of teamwork, information gathering and sharing across the organization, and risk management. To emphasize this shift, top management revised their process to place these competencies first on the performance plan, putting the technical results second. This change showed the criticality of driving these behaviors through the organization. Similarly, they separated out an overall rating of the competencies from the rating of results. Only those who achieved results while demonstrating the appropriate levels of those key competencies could earn the larger bonus.

CHAPTER 7

WHAT ARE THE TRAPS?

Chapter Overview

Organizations face an important choice today—one that can determine how rapidly they respond to a changing marketplace. It's a choice that leads to their vision and values being carried out and that gains their people's commitment to strategic goals. It's a choice that leads people to look at not only what to achieve, but how to achieve it. In essence, it's a choice that sets the framework for how people manage their performance.

It comes down to this: The organization can lead through fear and frustration, or it can lead through focus and flexibility.

It's that simple, really. Does the organization choose to manage associates via a typical performance appraisal process, which conjures fear and frustration in the minds of managers and associates alike? Or, does the organization opt for an almost-perfect performance management system— an empowering vehicle fueled by focus and flexibility? Such a system:

- Drives strategic direction and organizational change.
- Focuses people on high-payoff activities that make the organization more competitive.
- Promotes individual and team growth, participation, and commitment.

The solution, like the choice, seems basic. Reality, though, tells a different story.

The Five Traps

Most performance appraisal processes fail. Many organizations change these systems every four or five years, weary from poor results. These transitions result in yet another cycle of hope, frustration, and dissatisfaction. Unfortunately, the only thing the new systems guarantee is more change.

Before organizations can break this cycle, they must recognize the five traps associated with appraisal processes.

1. **Appraisal processes focus people on "filling out forms" instead of managing their daily performance.**

   Some organizations believe their associates' having a better form can correct existing problems. Granted, organizations need a way to document performance levels and summarize data. But when completing forms is more important than managing performance, the process is doomed. An effective performance management system, however, encourages managers and associates to work together, communicate openly, and provide feedback regularly. Until people focus on communication, cooperation, and collaboration skills, appraisal forms remain vehicles for failure, and appraisals go on evoking fear and suspicion.

2. **Performance appraisals serve as crutches for making compensation decisions rather than tools for developing people's abilities.**

   Many compensation committees develop processes, such as forced distribution techniques, that steer leaders away from the real issue—managing people's performance and their contributions to the organization. No performance management system can replace the need for managers to make tough decisions about performance. Yet, organizations waste millions of dollars trying to minimize a responsibility for which managers should earn their pay—making difficult decisions about performance. It's true that managers typically skew performance evaluations to the positive side. Or, they place everyone at the midpoint (central tendency). However, these are correctable problems if senior management is willing to establish situational controls that provide managers with straightforward feedback.

3. **Top-down implementation of performance appraisal processes minimizes people's involvement.**

   Too often, senior management sets goals and objectives without offering rationale as to why they are important. In many cases, associates do not take part in establishing these goals. An effective performance management system encourages information sharing, with associates providing ongoing, honest feedback on objectives, resources, ideas, marketplace conditions, competition, and product and service quality. This approach helps senior management set realistic, achievable targets that are based on associates' input. Involving people not only in setting objectives, but also in tracking and reviewing performance is extremely empowering. High levels of associate involvement often make the difference between an annual performance appraisal process and an effective, ongoing performance management system.

4. **Most performance appraisal processes focus on either *what* results are achieved or *how* they are achieved—but not both.**

   Performance is a combination of individual or team behaviors (the hows) directed toward specific goals or targets (the whats). Managing and measuring performance requires a balance between these quantifiable objectives and the more elusive behavioral expectations. Many management-by-objectives systems of the past failed because they ignored how people got their jobs done; instead, they focused solely on what was achieved. As a result, organizations made performance decisions based exclusively on results or lack of results. They didn't consider the behaviors or skills people used in trying to achieve those objectives. Consequently, organizations promoted people for the wrong reasons and, during bad times, let people go for similarly wrong reasons. How an organization achieves its objectives is as important as what it achieves. Balancing the what and how helps organizations get a complete picture of performance.

5. **Performance appraisal processes, particularly in matrixed organizations, do not clarify specific accountabilities.**

   Organizations must clarify accountabilities when they design performance management systems. Joint accountability usually means a job won't get done. Yet, many matrixed organizations have joint accountabilities, and confusion reigns in determining who is ultimately responsible for completing the work. The new wave in teams job design compounds the problem. For example, a large chemical company identifies gross margins as a joint responsibility of marketing and sales. Marketing personnel set the price margin, but salespeople change the price when needed to make a sale. While both departments are accountable, neither has the authority to control the outcome. Only clear-cut roles and accountabilities increase the probability of objectives being accomplished.

CHAPTER 8

STICKY ISSUES

Chapter Overview

The stickiest issue with performance management is the rating process and its link to compensation. Throughout this book we've talked about engagement, involvement, associate ownership of performance, and other vital aspects of an effective process. But how do you get all those and still use the data to make compensation decisions or other critical choices that affect people's careers, such as promotion and placement? The sticky issue of how to link performance to pay is one that organizations have struggled with for years. The bad news is there is no magic answer—it's hard work. Some companies have gone to forced-distribution systems, while others have integrated multirater results into the pay decision. In either situation we would say be careful—you might not get the results you want. Read on.

What About Forced Ranking?

Downsizing, cost-cutting, and a perception among senior executives that managers fail to adequately deal with substandard and mediocre performance have all led to the rising popularity of various techniques to address these issues. These controversial management tools target the "C" performers—those who, through their lack of productivity, motivation, and effectiveness, contribute the least to an organization's bottom line.

As strong proponents of performance management, we emphatically support the need for managers to do a better job of filtering out their lower-performing associates. We also understand that managers are reluctant to address substandard performance, either because of a lack of competence or confidence. After all, most of us are not thrilled when we have to deliver less-than-favorable news to an associate.

Consequently, senior leaders have embraced various techniques to force managers to differentiate among associates based on performance and to take action on those who rate lower. We wholeheartedly support this approach—the need is clearly evident. Not doing so results in "mediocrity creep" and a loss of faith and trust in senior executives by the organization's top performers.

We contend that there is a better way to get leaders to manage all associates—high and low performers alike—than to resort to organizationwide forced distribution or forced-ranking systems. The solution is a performance management system that supports the organization's strategic priorities by promoting constant, open, and honest feedback between leaders and associates and by building managers' competence and confidence in how to conduct these most difficult discussions.

Forced Ranking: A Closer Look

But, first, let's review forced ranking and why some organizations are adopting it even while others are sweeping the program into the dustbin of failed evaluation systems.

Former General Electric chief Jack Welch, an enthusiastic supporter of forced ranking, called the practice "the vitality curve." It's also known as "top grading," "forced distribution," and "cut-to-build strategy." Whatever it's called, forced ranking is seen by leaders in a growing number of organizations as a handy grading tool for creating a high-performing culture. In their view, forced ranking better enables leaders to manage low performers. GE's success in implementing a forced-ranking system is cited as the model by many of the 20 percent of U.S. companies that have adopted it in recent years. (At General Electric each year, 10 percent of managers are assigned the bottom grade; if they don't improve, they are asked to move on.)

What's behind this popularity? Generally, forced ranking is being adopted because senior leaders believe their managers have not addressed performance problems or adequately developed their staffs' talent. These leaders believe that forced ranking will help managers who are not doing their jobs to raise the level of performance in their organizations.

Its proponents maintain that forced ranking addresses two issues that are key to building a high-performing organizational culture. First, it encourages managers to identify and remove poor performers. Second, it forces a predetermined compensation distribution curve, which allows managers to handsomely reward top performers, while encouraging weak performers to leave the organization.

Philosophically, DDI supports the desired results, but not the process. Even Jack Welch is aware of the need to be sensitive to cultural issues. He recently stated that the GE vitality curve can't simply be dropped into an organization if that organization isn't set up culturally for the implementation. W. James McNerney, Jr., one of Welch's senior executives at GE, found this to be all too true when he was at 3M. He'd been 3M's chief executive for 18 months before he felt he could implement a similar system.

Success at GE and 3M can't mask the fact that the adoption of forced ranking has not been without its problems. A rash of lawsuits has forced many organizations to reconsider using forced ranking. For example, Ford Motor Company's system graded associates "A," "B," or "C," with an initial requirement that 10 percent of the population be graded a "C." The intent was simple: Remove poor performers. Instead, the automaker landed in court. Eventually, after six lawsuits were filed against Ford by disgruntled workers, former CEO Jacques Nasser announced that the unpopular grading system was being modified.

One Manager's Experience

For some companies the perceived benefits of forced ranking are far outweighed by its drawbacks. It often results in low morale stemming from associates competing against instead of working with one another. Furthermore, many associates believe that their continued employment rests not on what they do, but on who supports them. The belief that your survival in a forced ranking system boils down to your leader's effectiveness as an advocate for his or her associates can undermine the entire organization. This point is borne out by the following account, provided by a leader who has managed in a forced distribution system.

> *My experience as a manager (in a forced-ranking system) revealed that a leader's communication skills and credibility have more to do with an associate's rank than does the associate's performance. For instance, we had one manager who was trained in behaviorally based assessment skills. These skills made it possible for him to be more convincing when advocating for his associates than other managers who lacked the same skill set. In three years of observing this manager, I never saw him lower a ranking for one of his associates. If all managers were trained as this manager was, then forced ranking would provide a level playing field in which associates could be placed in the right categories of performance. But this requires a culture that is prepped for the implementation of a forced-ranking system. The organization I worked for did not have such a system in place, so adopting forced ranking resulted in culture shock. People were less willing to help others whom they would be ranked against. Associates were more eager to pass on to senior executives negative information about others. And people lobbied for assignments to corporate headquarters because they saw that those who worked closely with senior executives received consistently higher rankings.*

Within one year this worldwide organization changed its system, as Ford did, to take the onus off the 10 percent at the bottom. This account echoes Jack Welch's comments that the missing key in this and other failed examples is a corporate culture that can successfully absorb a forced-ranking system. GE had such a culture, one based on honest feedback supported by a performance management system.

The value that Welch placed on open and honest feedback at GE is illustrated in this question he asked one conference audience: "How many of you work for a company with integrity?" A sea of raised hands indicated that almost all thought they did. He then asked, "How many of you get straight, honest feedback about your performance?" Very few hands went up. That response, he said, supported his conclusion that unless an organization promotes the giving of honest, straightforward feedback at every level, then it did not have integrity. Only in those very rare organizations that have extremely high levels of integrity can forced distribution systems even have a chance to succeed. We believe there are better alternatives.

The Prescription

The lesson to be learned from Welch's argument is that, used alone as a management tool, forced ranking does not guarantee success. In fact, in most cases the so-called "cure" of forced ranking could be worse than the "illness" of weak performers. The alternative is one that should have been prescribed in the first place—a performance management system that:

- Holds associates accountable for results.
- Encourages and supports open, honest feedback between associates at all levels.
- Provides a convenient mechanism for developing talent.
- Features a compensation process that is based on performance and pays the high performers more than it pays substandard performers.

It's not unreasonable for organizations to want their managers to handle performance problems, develop talent, make tough decisions about removing poor performers, and distribute pay equitably. All this can be done without implementing a controversial ranking system. So, why aren't managers managing their staffs? Most likely, it's because they face one or more of the following barriers:

- Their organization does not have a good performance management system in place.
- Leaders lack the competence or confidence needed to set performance expectations, provide feedback, and deal with performance problems.
- Leaders are not held accountable for substandard performance or for dealing with substandard performers.

- The organization's compensation system does not require leaders to make tough decisions.

The "Good" in Good Performance Management

Let's address the first barrier. By "good performance management system," we mean one that:

- Establishes clearly defined performance objectives for all associates. These objectives should support the organization's efforts to achieve higher levels of performance from one year to the next.

- Includes competencies (that is, knowledge, skills, and behaviors) needed to achieve the organization's business results in every associate's performance plan and defines those competencies behaviorally. For example, every leader's plan should include the Developing Talent competency. In turn, the behavioral expectations for Developing Talent should include continuously developing associates, setting challenging performance expectations for staff, monitoring progress against expectations, and addressing performance gaps. To be evaluated "effective" in Developing Talent, a leader must successfully demonstrate each of these behaviors.

- Features an individual development plan for every associate. The development plan should identify competencies the associate needs to improve in his or her current role or for a future role. The plan also should include specific development objectives that will enhance performance in the assigned competencies.

Improving Managers' Competence and Confidence

As for the second barrier, even the best-designed performance management system won't be effective if managers lack the competence and confidence to use it. Training is essential if all associates—but especially leaders—are to understand and use a performance management system. Although organizations generally understand this truism, all too many focus their training on the mechanics of the process, such as completing the appraisal document. While this kind of training is necessary, managers would be better served if their training focused on writing measurable objectives, assessing and evaluating competencies, and interacting effectively with peers, direct reports, and others.

These interaction skills will enable managers to effectively reach agreement on performance expectations, provide honest feedback, coach associates who are not performing at expected levels, communicate the consequences of not improving poor performance, and conduct review discussions that encourage associates to sustain good performance and improve where needed. The absence of these interaction skills, on the other hand, can be disastrous.

We studied a large division of a company that thought it was "successfully" using a ranking system. However, we found widespread associate dissatisfaction, managers who simply went "through the motions," and a human resources department flooded with complaints from people who weren't getting the coaching and feedback they needed to improve their performance. Our diagnosis revealed that, although all managers were trained in the system, they were not trained in the interaction skills they needed to conduct performance discussions. The system turned out to be not such a success after all.

Top Leaders Have a Role Too

The third barrier—managers not being held accountable for substandard performance—is an issue for an organization's top leaders. Senior executives must hold leaders accountable for substandard performance and for improving or removing poor performers. In performance discussions with direct reports, senior executives should identify the weaker performers, analyze the cause of poor performance (lack of motivation or skill, poor job fit, etc.), and reach agreement with the direct reports on improvement goals or redeployment options. If an associate must be removed from a position, managers need the organization's support as they counsel the associate to leave the company or help him or her find a more suitable position within it. In short, it is critical that senior executives use the performance management system to hold their managers accountable for carrying out the necessary employment actions.

Alternatives to Forced Ranking

The fourth barrier—lacking a compensation system that requires managers to allocate more to high performers and less to substandard performers— might be the toughest problem to solve. While there are ways to manage compensation besides resorting to a forced-ranking system, such alternatives can be very challenging.

We've observed or helped clients with the following alternatives to forced-distribution systems:

- A compensation/HR committee reviews merit pay raises and bonuses against unit and individual performance.

- Senior line managers are held accountable for distributing a pool of funds based on performance as well as for tracking all managers' pay decisions to identify problems (such as central tendency, favoritism, and discrimination).

- A senior line manager reviews all pay decisions in his or her department to ensure alignment with the pay-for-performance approach.

- Senior line managers randomly examine performance reviews and related pay increases. The senior line managers at LaSalle Bank in Chicago look at as many as 160 performance reviews a year to ensure that they are completed and that the quality of the reviews and pay increases is aligned with the record of individual performance.
- Internal and external third parties evaluate performance and alignment to pay.

These methods show that it's possible to bring the same rigor and discipline to managing the "C" performers without the downsides found in a forced-distribution system. However, they all require that managers *manage,* which brings us full circle to the crux of the issue.

When an effective performance management system is combined with a compensation management process, the results can be the same as those sought in a forced-distribution system, but without the negative effects. Instead of looking for a crutch, organizations need to set clear expectations and hold leaders accountable for achieving them in addition to tracking performance and providing coaching and honest feedback.

By doing so, the organization's human resource management processes will have integrity. After all, wasn't that the objective all the while?

Multirater Feedback and Performance Management

As DDI's 2003 performance management survey (Bernthal, Rogers, & Smith) indicated, 19 percent of the respondent organizations have integrated multirater (also known as 360°) feedback processes into their performance management system. (See the Merck case study in chapter 9.) The rationale behind this integration is that the more and diverse input an organization can get on an individual's performance, the more accurate the performance evaluation will be. In theory, it certainly sounds logical and rational. In fact, we heartily support using multiple inputs into a performance management process. However, we believe that very few organizations will take all the necessary steps when using a multirater survey output as performance data to ensure the accuracy of the data. Multirater/360° instruments generate results that are useful indicators and can, indeed, alert management to problem areas or major strengths. But that awareness should be followed up with fact finding to confirm the problem area or strength before drawing final conclusions. For development purposes multirater results remain very useful feedback mechanisms. But to use 360° results as gospel or to determine performance ratings that drive pay or promotion decisions would be simply unfair to the individuals using the instrument. Let's examine why that is our position.

There are many issues regarding the accuracy of multirater instruments. Most, if not all, multirater instruments tell us how someone is *perceived*— not necessarily how someone actually behaves or how skilled that person is. Although this perception does not necessarily equate to a person's competency skill level, multirater instruments nonetheless ask the raters to evaluate a multitude of areas. This doesn't mean that we don't support the use of multirater instruments—we do. In fact, we require all DDI leaders to participate every 18 months in a multirater survey of their leadership. This ensures that they are getting regular feedback on how they are perceived by their direct reports and peers. This is a valuable process to help our leaders understand how they are affecting others around them. We use the results to focus on developing effective leadership skills for all our leaders. We don't, however, use the data to conduct performance evaluations, merit pay discussions, or other personnel decisions. Here are the questions about multirater instruments that must be asked each time an instrument is used.

1. **Are the competencies/dimensions and behaviors to be rated the right ones for the individual?** Are the areas to be rated observable in the individual roles, and are they relevant to the individual's current duties and responsibilities? Or is it a standard list that everyone gets rated on, whether they have an opportunity to demonstrate the behaviors or not?

2. **If they are a standard list of behaviors to be rated, are the raters trained in what to observe and how to rate each area?** What standards have been established? What training of the rating process has occurred? How do you prevent raters from inflating the ratings (the most common occurrence) or deflating the ratings because of differences in standards if none have been established? DDI's 2003 research (Bernthal, Rogers, & Smith) in this area found that only 35 percent of the organizations surveyed felt that peer management and direct reports' input to performance reviews were at least adequately effective.

3. **Do the raters have an opportunity to observe the person demonstrating the behaviors they are being asked to rate?** How often do you see a direct report coach, delegate, run a meeting, explain accountabilities, etc.? Suppose the boss works in a different location, or even in a different country. In these cases you would probably never see the person exhibiting many of the behaviors you would be asked to rate him or her on. Although most multirater instruments allow a "not observed" response, we have seen few raters use it.

4. **How do you prevent a multirater instrument from becoming a popularity contest?** Who chooses the raters? If the person being rated gets to choose the raters and the results affect personnel decisions, it is a sure bet that bias is alive and well in your system. How could it not be? In our own company, although we use multirater surveys only for

development, we still insist that the manager of the person being rated helps to select the raters. How highly will you be rated by someone you just put on probation for poor performance? Or, suppose you just promoted someone—it's very likely that person will give you high marks in judgment—don't you think?

For the reasons just mentioned and probably a few more, multirater instruments must be implemented with extreme care if you want to ensure that the process produces fair results and doesn't create more problems in the long run. The biggest problem we've encountered with multirater implementations is that everyone's ratings are significantly inflated, which actually stifles development because people get an inflated perception of their capabilities.

Two Real-Life Examples

Two real-life examples will help to make the point that you have to be very diligent and careful in implementing and drawing conclusions from multirater instruments.

The first example occurred when we were giving feedback to a CEO of a worldwide chemical company's U.S. division. The feedback from his senior leadership team in the U.S. indicated that he was very weak in decision making. This CEO had been a CFO for a large European division of the company, had had extensive experience in the financial area, and had held management positions at the corporate headquarters in the United Kingdom. We had worked with the CEO for more than a year, helping him with strategic priorities, leadership development, and a performance management implementation. During the course of our work, it became apparent that this CEO was not at all weak in analysis nor decision making. We saw his very thorough analysis, his careful consideration of alternatives, and a logical, sound basis for his eventual decisions. Understandably, the CEO was confused by the 360° ratings. We explained that while we didn't believe he was low in decision making, he was doing something that made a significant number of his direct reports believe that he was.

After considerable discussion and looking at other areas in the survey, we arrived at two insights that helped to explain the low rating. First, when he was new in the position, he wanted the group to make some major changes he believed were necessary. The group strongly resented a number of those changes although they were the right things to do. Second, this CEO was not strong in communication; he tended not to share his rationale and reasoning for the decisions he made. Consequently, many of his direct reports didn't see his perspective or understand where he was coming from. When we looked at some of these behaviors under the Communication competency, we also found low ratings. We had uncovered the developmental area, and it wasn't decision making at all!

The second example is a similar situation for one of the heads of a large U.S. board of trade. The challenge here was even greater, as the 360° survey indicated that this chairman was low in integrity. After a lengthy discussion of this factor, it became clear that he wasn't low on integrity at all, but that some of his behaviors were creating that impression in others. Again, we focused on the behaviors that had created that impression and helped him modify what he was doing, which subsequently eliminated the false perception.

In both cases, perceptions were created that were not accurate in terms of skills, but were a reflection of how each person was coming across. In both cases the feedback was very useful in getting the senior leaders to modify their behaviors to stop creating that perception. One could argue that perception is reality. Our argument has always been that this is true with customers, but not necessarily so with direct reports due to the likelihood of biases, likes, dislikes, etc. If a customer thinks you are not responsive—then that perception becomes the reality you must change. If not, your business results will suffer. With direct reports or peers, you should still work on changing the perceptions as long as the raters weren't influenced by their own biases or beliefs and they don't necessarily indicate an accurate measure of skill or knowledge.

The following case study shows how BASF leveraged a 360° survey to focus its leaders' attention on what specific competencies they might develop in the context of a companywide leadership training curriculum.

case study

BASF CORPORATION

BASF, the North American affiliate of the BASF Group in Ludwigshafen, Germany, serves several industries. BASF is committed to improving its entire spectrum of chemicals, coatings, plastics, fibers, and health and nutrition products to meet global market and customer demands.

To maintain industry leadership and promote constant improvement, the information systems group (NTI) at BASF decided to implement a high-involvement culture over several years. Introducing such a culture would be a complex process, involving revisiting skills, systems, accountabilities, and communications.

While all these changes could occur simultaneously, each required a different intervention, and each change needed a unique approach. NTI took on the challenge of implementing organizational changes that were driven by BASF's vision and values.

Because change requires new ways of thinking and strong leadership, NTI introduced a program targeted specifically at improving leader competencies (that is, skills, knowledge, and behaviors). NTI created a training curriculum, the Leadership Academy, to address the skills component of the culture change. When combined with other changes, training programs can develop the skills necessary to produce a high-involvement culture. The Leadership Academy objectives included developing:

- Individual and team leadership.
- A strategic, customer-focused approach.
- Tactical and business skills.

By implementing a program that balanced these three skill areas, NTI hoped to improve all the behaviors necessary for strong leadership. Leaders in the program participated in a three-week learning experience preceded by a 360° assessment.

This is an ideal example of how to use a 360° assessment. Rather than employing a multirater instrument once a year or using it as a means to provide feedback on general performance criteria, BASF used it to focus leaders' attention on the specific competencies that were to be the subject of the Leadership Academy. This approach fixed leaders' concentration on the training to come. As a result, the Academy has been an unqualified success.

The Results

- **A good investment.** The Leadership Academy has been well received by participants. Leaders who were asked to rate program value were very pleased. A vast majority, 90 percent, of the leaders said their confidence in using the behaviors increased at least moderately.

- **Competency acquisition.** The Academy helped leaders acquire proficiency in nine competencies important for a high-involvement culture.

- **Significant behavior change.** Participation in the Academy has led to improvement of the behaviors needed for a high-involvement culture. Leaders and their coworkers rated leaders' use of the behaviors before and after training. The results showed a statistically significant improvement in all the targeted behaviors. The greatest changes were seen in the leaders' ability to champion empowerment.

BASF CORPORATION (cont'd)

- **Improved work environment.** The Leadership Academy led to positive changes in the culture during its first year. Although initial results were encouraging, there is still room for improvement. So far, the greatest improvements have been seen in terms of responsiveness, focus, and solution orientation. Long-term culture change will take additional time. To facilitate additional change, a greater emphasis is needed on accountability and follow-up for leaders' use of appropriate behaviors.

Linking Compensation and Performance Management

Here goes nothing! Time for raises. You'd think I'd be happy, but as a manager, I dread it. I have to divide my pot of money among my group in a way that will create the least conflict possible, but reward people accordingly too. And, oh yes, provide written documentation to HR for each raise. And, of course, explain to each person why he or she got what raise. So much for the "fun" part of my job.

Does that quote from an insurance company manager sound familiar? A lot of organizations work this way. They use their performance management system as a way of helping people meet individual, departmental, and organizational goals, and to determine who earns what pay raises. Seems like a logical use for a performance management system. But is the system really designed for that purpose? Hardly.

There are some ways, however, to tie performance management to compensation without defeating the purpose of either. The keys to this and any successful relationship are open communication and fair practices.

At DDI we've worked with organizations, big and small, across a wide variety of industries to design performance management systems that help people reach peak performance. When companies want to link performance management to compensation, one of the first questions that arises is, "Should salary and raises be discussed during the performance review or not?" We suggest that the two discussions be separated, with the performance review occurring at the end of the fiscal year and the salary review on the associate's hire anniversary date. This allows leaders to focus on the performance data without being distracted by pay issues. Obviously, performance should be taken into account when making pay decisions; however, other factors such as the following might enter into salary decisions as well:

- External market competitiveness.

- Job worth to the organization.

- Where a person falls within a salary range.
- Salary history (time since last increase, size of last increase, etc.).
- Supervisor-direct report pay relationships.
- Internal pay equity.
- Labor contracts.
- Cost-of-living changes.
- The organization's financial picture, including profitability and salary budgets.

Whether salary discussions are held separate from or along with performance reviews, one thing is certain: Successful performance management and compensation systems thrive on trust and open communication. Much of the skill building around a successful performance management system is designed to help people develop trusting relationships. The same is true for compensation. People need to feel comfortable sharing information openly— especially when it comes to money. Sharing information such as salary ranges, salary market survey data, merit budget guidelines, and company finances helps build knowledge, understanding, and trust.

Despite the relationship between the performance management and compensation systems, we think it best not to restructure them at the same time because people might think that raises and bonuses are based solely on the performance management system. If both systems need to be restructured, build a solid performance management system first, and then change the compensation system later. The key to both systems is *alignment*. Performance management is a powerful business tool that helps organizations achieve their vision, values, and strategic business objectives. Likewise, effective pay programs should communicate organizational values and goals. If pay, reward, and benefit systems align with the organization's cultural and business strategies, the systems can help the organization perform better and also help attract, develop, and retain high-caliber employees.

Why Not Base Pay Raises on Ratings or Forced Ranking?

When starting a new performance management system, many clients ask us for advice on how to handle ratings, believing they can be used to determine pay increases. In particular, many clients think an overall rating of someone's performance or a forced ranking, in which people are slotted into a set ranking among coworkers, can help with pay issues. Sounds reasonable, right? Well, here are two reasons why organizations should consider *not* using these approaches.

- Think about the amount of work you do in a year—the time and energy you invest in day-to-day tasks, not to mention any special projects that need your attention. Then imagine how you would feel if your manager sat down with you at the end of the year and said, "Well, you did a good job this year. I'm giving you a performance rating of 3." What does that mean? The overall rating attempts to sum up individual performance with a number. But a single number does not reflect strengths, accomplishments, or development needs. Such an approach is inaccurate and unfair and often lowers a person's self-esteem, which certainly doesn't help people perform at their best. Some organizations go to great lengths to develop elaborate formulas that lead to a bottom-line number tied to a salary increase. This sort of formula gives a false sense of precision and minimizes the value of discussing performance in the broader terms of key accomplishments, strengths, and developmental areas.

  The *summary statement* is a much better way to evaluate performance. It describes a person's accomplishments, contributions to the organization, key strengths, and areas for improvement. This information can be used for HR decisions, including compensation, and more accurately reflects people's value and potential.

  Compare your perceptions of an overall "3" or a "consistently meets objectives" rating with a summary statement such as this one:

  Sam's performance in this business year has had a significant impact on his unit's success. Major accomplishments included leading his team in delivering four large client projects, meeting all deadlines, and eliciting high levels of customer satisfaction. The gross margins on three of the four projects exceeded company standards due to Sam's diligence in monitoring expenses and his creative problem solving when the client requested items that weren't in the original specs. Sam's leadership skills were clearly evident as he managed a disruptive associate on his team out of the company. Sam could improve his performance by expanding his experience and knowledge of our largest product lines. This would enable him to lead larger, more complex client projects. Sam is a valuable member of our leadership team who should be able to handle additional responsibilities in the future.

- Imagine you are supervising five people in a work group. All are performing equally well, but you must rank them from one to five to divvy up compensation dollars. Such a forced ranking is unfair—to employees and their managers. In fact, DDI's 2003 managing performance survey (Bernthal, Rogers, & Smith) showed that many respondents cited an informal forced ranking system as their major source of frustration with their organization's performance management system. This sort of system often results in people competing against, instead of working with, one another.

Why do organizations go to such extremes of developing forced rankings, overall ratings, or weighting systems? Usually, because the performance appraisal serves as a crutch for making compensation decisions rather than as a tool for managing performance and developing people's abilities. No performance management system can replace the need for managers to make tough decisions about performance. Yet, organizations waste millions of dollars trying to minimize a responsibility for which managers should earn their pay—making difficult decisions about performance. The reality is that there is no magic formula for tough decision making. But it can be made easier by using a performance management system that is based on behavior and accomplishments that are clearly agreed upon at the beginning of the performance cycle and that are jointly tracked and evaluated throughout the year.

Compensation Basics

What is the right compensation program for your organization? The answer is, "It depends." It depends on many factors: business strategy, need for organizational flexibility, industry and labor market practices and trends, associate input and preferences, fixed versus variable pay combinations, organizational structure (for example, flat versus multiple levels, team performance versus individual performance), and many other factors. To make an informed decision, organizations should first analyze market and industry data, employee input and preferences, and strategic business needs—including the outcomes or results they need from their compensation and reward systems. After such analysis the organization is ready to establish a compensation philosophy and a core set of operating principles and practices. There are many options that organizations can choose from when designing their systems, including merit pay, incentive pay, individual bonuses, gain sharing, profit sharing, and team bonuses, to name a few. But that's for another book.

How Do Performance Management Systems Link to Pay?

All organizations set objectives or goals, but regardless of whether these objectives are met or not met depends upon that important key: *alignment.* An effective performance management system ensures that individual and team performance objectives reflect organizational objectives—that they are aligned. All individuals should be trained in how to clearly define *what* and *how* objectives, which together represent individual and team performance. When they are used correctly, performance management systems make a difference in organizational effectiveness, including improved profit margins, increased sales, and reduced cycle time for bringing products to market. Organizations using profit-sharing and gain-sharing incentive programs, combined with an effective performance management system, should see higher payouts (resulting from higher profits).

Because merit pay seems to be a very popular method for determining base salary increases, here are some examples of how merit pay increases might be determined using performance data:

Option 1: Establish guidelines for the range of increases throughout the organization—for example 0–6 percent. Hold managers who supervise a minimum of 25–30 associates to an average of x percent (in recent years these have averaged 2–4 percent due to low inflation rates). Set guidelines for levels of performance (Exceeds, Meets, or Below Expectations) and associated pay increase levels. For example, "Below Expectations" gets 0–2 percent, "Meets Expectations" gets 3–4 percent, and "Exceeds Expectations" gets 5–6 percent. Allow exceptions for market-equity corrections only.

Option 2: Determine the overall level of performance (see guidelines above). Compare the associate's current salary level to the existing range for the position. Place the associate's salary level in the top, middle, or bottom third of the range. Using a matrix like the one in Table 8.1, identify the appropriate merit pay increase.

Table 8.1: Sample Salary Matrix

Salary Range

	Top Third	Middle Third	Bottom Third
Exceeds Expectations	4–6%	6–8%	8–10%
Meets Expectations	3–5%	4–6%	5–7%
Below Expectations	0–3%	0–3%	0–3%

Option 3: Install a forced-distribution system that allows only certain percentages to be rated in each performance category. Then merit pay increases can be set for each level.

Performance management also can be easily linked to incentive pay in a variety of ways. A successful organization depends on the contributions of each associate. And each associate has important areas of responsibility, also known as key result areas (KRAs), that describe the expected results of a job and that reflect organizational values. By achieving specific objectives within a KRA, a person helps the organization reach its overall goals.

In terms of incentive pay, bonuses can be linked to the achievement of such objectives. It is also possible to link the bonus to the overall KRA results (usually encompassing the achievement of multiple objectives) or competency ratings. Bonuses may be deflated if performance in a particular dimension of importance, such as Collaboration, is lower than acceptable.

Bonuses also can be based on overall results for two KRAs in a matrix format, such as the one shown in Table 8.2. In this instance "customer service" might be based on internal and external customer service scorecard results, meeting customer project timelines, and the achievement of other objectives related to customer service. "Profit" could be based on required gross margin (by project or projects) versus actual.

Table 8.2: A Bonus Matrix Based on Customer Satisfaction and Profit

		Profit				
		1	2	3	4	5
Customer Satisfaction	5	0	80	120	130	140
	4	0	80	110	120	130
	3	0	80	100	110	120
	2	0	50	80	80	80
	1	0	0	0	0	0

Performance, Pay, and Perception

Regardless of what system or process you use, the true test will be whether associates think the compensation system is based on performance factors and whether they perceive it to be fair. The better the performance management system is at involving associates and the more accurate the feedback and, consequently, the evaluation of performance, the fairer associates will think the system is—and the fewer complaints you'll get about compensation. Make no mistake—these are not easy results to achieve. But they *can* be achieved.

PART III

The Power of Realization

CHAPTER 9

GETTING TO REALIZATION

Chapter Overview

One of the most difficult human resource systems to implement effectively is the performance management system. Yet, almost every organization has one. The heart of the issue is this: What must organizations do to ensure effectiveness, that is, produce the desired results that truly improve performance across the company? In other words, how do they achieve *realization*?

Achieving realization isn't easy. It takes considerable time and energy to ensure that the performance management system becomes more than an administrative headache.

Implementing a performance management system that will produce the desired results consists of five steps:

1. Make the business case/Communicate the need.
2. Establish clear roles and accountabilities for all stakeholders.
3. Develop the skills of all participants.
4. Align systems and processes.
5. Provide clear measures.

Five Steps to Realization

Read on to learn how following these five steps will enable you to reap the results you're hoping to see.

1. Make the business case/Communicate the need.

When implementing a new performance management system, it's critical for an organization to develop a pre-launch, launch, and post-launch communication plan. Multiple communication vehicles should be used, such as newsletters, Internet information flashes, posters, letters from the CEO and other executives, voice mails, e-mails, videos, brochures, user handbooks, reminders attached to pay stubs, Q&A

hotlines, mandatory training, refresher training, etc. Communications should be crafted to build enthusiasm, understanding, and commitment by continually emphasizing to associates, leaders, and the organization the benefits of using the system.

The communications also need to continually demonstrate that leaders on the senior executive team are articulate advocates who are passionate about using the new system and who are continually extolling the value and importance of the system to the organization and to all associates. We have seen our clients use a variety of techniques to promote senior-leader advocacy of their performance management systems, including:

- Identifying a senior executive sponsor who has accountability for owning the performance management system and keeping it alive and well.
- Having senior executives randomly audit performance plans and provide coaching when quality problems are identified.
- Cascading strategic priorities from mid-level managers down to individual contributors.
- Identifying specific objectives in each senior executive's plan that support the continued use of the system.
- Establishing a "hot line" through which questions can be asked and answered.
- Providing online tools and refresher tips.
- Training all new leaders in the process within their first month on the job.
- Tying bonuses to the quality and timeliness of performance reviews within each vice president's functional area.
- Publishing senior vice presidents' performance plans and performance reviews.
- Including performance management system best practices and implementation issues as ongoing agenda items in monthly senior management meetings.

Only by constantly advocating, cajoling, recognizing, rewarding, and encouraging any and all associates to use the performance management system effectively will the message be clear: Using the system is mission critical, and the senior executive team is 150 percent behind it.

2. Establish clear roles and accountabilities for all stakeholders.

A performance management system, in and of itself, is an accountability system. It shows everyone, from senior executives to frontline associates, what business results they are accountable for and sets expectations for how they should go about achieving those results. To be implemented effectively, the process needs to start at the top. Senior executives need to clearly define the organization's strategic priorities and communicate them throughout the organization. The strategic priorities are the "make or break," action-oriented targets the organization must focus on in order to move toward its vision— such as improving the customer retention rate or accelerating its products' speed to market. One of our clients identified the long-term implementation of a new performance management system as one of its strategic priorities. That created the focus the organization needed to help ensure its success.

Once the priorities are defined, the senior executive team needs to establish measures for them. Using the balanced scorecard approach— including both lead and lag measures—is an excellent way to establish organizational measures. The lead and lag measures then should be integrated into the senior executives' performance objectives. Using the performance management system, senior executives then need to transfer accountabilities to the next level down. And the process continues down throughout the entire organization. For example:

- A large banking institution has its high-priority objectives posted on its intranet. From those high-priority objectives, the organization established business unit, departmental, and unit objectives, and then cascaded them into individual performance plans, starting at the executive level.

- Milton Hershey School cascades objectives from a five-year strategic plan. From the strategic plan, an annual plan is written for each division or school, and from that, objectives are cascaded into individual plans.

- Briggs & Stratton Corporation starts the cascading process with its EVA (Economic Value Added) measures, which are cascaded into each plant's goals, then rolled down to the department level, the team level, and finally to specific shifts of workers.

The senior executive team also can use the performance management system to hold people accountable for its implementation. For instance, a utility company uses the system to ensure that the performance management process is effectively implemented. The company requires that all leaders have mandated objectives that they are evaluated against for conducting reaching-agreement discussions, interim review discussions, and year-end review discussions—all within specified timelines. Another example is a large insurance company that rolled out its performance management system by setting the expectation that all its managers would conduct quarterly discussions. When they received training in the new system, leaders were encouraged to incorporate discussions into their quarterly one-on-one meetings, making them a part of their normal routine rather than an additional responsibility. This approach has proven highly successful, making the performance management system a living, breathing entity and not a one-time, year-end review process.

3. **Develop the skills of all participants.**

In any installation of a process intended to change behavior, it's critical to develop all associates' confidence and competence in fulfilling their new roles. An effective performance management system actively involves associates throughout the performance cycle. Managers don't develop performance plans for their associates; instead, they give associates business unit information and the manager's objectives so the associates can then draft their own plans. Associates track and share their performance data, allowing leaders to provide timely feedback to boost or reinforce performance. Associates self-rate their own performance and lead the performance review discussion.

This type of shared ownership requires skill development training for both leaders and associates. Both groups need to know their responsibilities in the process and how to:

- Create measurable objectives and observable competencies.
- Track performance.
- Seek, give, and receive feedback.
- Evaluate performance.
- Conduct effective performance discussions.

One of our client organizations understood the value of training all associates and took steps to ensure that the necessary training would occur. If all associates within a business unit did not comply, the senior vice president of that business unit became ineligible for his or her bonus.

4. **Align systems and processes.**

We have already discussed the importance of aligning the performance management system to support the organization's strategic priorities and business unit goals, but that is just the beginning of the alignment effort. It's also important to determine how other systems will support the performance management system and how data from it will be used to support other HR systems, such as training and development, succession planning, selection and promotion, rewards and recognition, and compensation. Following are two examples of how organizations successfully aligned performance management with other systems.

- A chemical manufacturing company identified a list of competencies that are important for success in specific positions representing a large number of associates. The company incorporated the evaluation of these competencies into the selection process for hiring people into those positions. When newly hired associates receive feedback from their hiring managers on the competency evaluations that were part of the screening process, they also begin to discuss those competencies that should have development objectives included in their performance plans. The new hires also determine which of the selection competencies will be most critical to include in their performance plans to track and evaluate. This practice provides an immediate link between the competencies used for selection and the competencies used to evaluate performance in the new job. The two systems are aligned and reinforce each other.

- A large manufacturing firm wanted to be sure that its compensation system struck a balance between competencies and individual performance plan objectives. The organization required that 40 percent of each associate's performance evaluation be based on the individual's competency ratings. The ensuing overall rating was then used to determine merit pay increases. Thus, the compensation increase reflected the importance of associates' effectively demonstrating competencies as evaluated in the performance management system. Again, each system supported the other.

Competencies can serve as the point of integration for all HR systems. As you review how performance data will be used in other HR systems, check for inconsistencies and address them. Make sure that the same competency database supports all systems.

5. **Provide clear measures.**

It's important to decide how you'll evaluate the effectiveness of a performance management system before you begin to implement it. What are the outcomes you want from the system, and how will you measure them? Initially, most organizations focus on monitoring compliance, because the first challenge is getting everyone to use the system.

For example, are performance plans, interim reviews and final reviews being completed on time? Often, HR will measure compliance, but it's best to give line managers the responsibility of improving those compliance measures. This can be done with reminders, by one-on-one coaching, or through even more drastic actions that have worked for some of our clients, such as publishing each manager's review-completion rate or withholding merit increases or bonuses for noncompliance. In one service organization a group of managers and associates conducted structured interviews and participated in focus groups to determine their performance management system's effectiveness. They discovered that managers who held mid-cycle reviews had considerably more buy-in and commitment from associates than managers who set expectations at the beginning of the year and conducted only a year-end review. After considerable data verified this result, the organization required that everyone conduct midyear reviews.

Once using the system becomes part of the culture, the focus of the evaluation process shifts to the quality and effectiveness of the system. Spot quality audits of performance plans and reviews, questions on associate satisfaction surveys and exit interviews, and links from system effectiveness to key business results all are measurement techniques that clients have found useful.

A large insurance company has its HR generalists review appraisals for quality, quantity, and consistency. Then they provide feedback to the functional area VP, who is tasked with coaching line managers in his or her business unit to improve system effectiveness. Another company used an upward appraisal process in which associates were asked to evaluate how effectively their managers used the system. Results were provided to the managers and their leaders and, when needed, improvement goals were put into the managers' next performance plans.

The following case study shows how Merck improved its performance management system by measuring its effectiveness, adjusting it accordingly, and monitoring the adjustments.

case study

MERCK

Merck remains one of the world's most respected companies. From its vision and purpose to its major human resource efforts, Merck has earned a reputation as a leader in practices and results. But, like many other organizations, one area in which Merck has struggled over the years has been performance management. In 2001 senior executives decided to try again to improve their system. They created a performance management action team comprising senior executives from various functions and divisions. To drive improvements in their system, the action team put its purpose in writing. The team was determined to:

- Recruit, retain, and develop the best and brightest people.
- Develop leadership capabilities at every level.
- Ensure flexibility to respond quickly to changing dynamics in their particular businesses.
- Create an environment that enhances diversity and removes barriers to success.

With extensive surveys in 1999 and 2000, they had identified several areas for improvement in the Merck performance management system:

- The system did not differentiate top performers from poor performers.
- In some divisions good practices were in place, but their usage was inconsistent.
- The Merck culture did not support addressing conflict nor providing direct feedback.
- Clear integration, alignment, and skill building were needed across all aspects of performance management.
- Performance management concerns were consistent across demographics.

Consequently, Merck's executives revised the system with a clear focus on improving the following components: the objective-setting process, the quality of dialog and feedback, accountability, the rating system, and the link to pay. Merck provided additional training and coaching in each of these areas while making significant changes in how feedback was solicited and how pay was linked to performance.

Already in place was the interim (midyear) review process, but Merck wanted better and multiple feedback sources to drive the sharper focus on development. In 2003 the organization automated a multirater tool for each associate that enhanced the quality of the feedback from multiple sources. Merck even customized the tool for senior executives to capture the complexities and challenges of senior leaders. In 2003 more than 125,000 multirater instruments were completed. The following year the process was rolled out to all divisions worldwide, with translations in seven different languages.

One of the most significant changes was elimination of the overall rating at year's end. According to Dr. Shirley Ross, vice president of talent management and organizational effectiveness, "Merck wanted to get away from a single overall performance label and focus the year-end review on achievement of objectives (whats) and expectations (hows)." She also stated that with better feedback and more familiarity in providing interim reviews, managers could focus the year-end review on clarifying associates' strengths and developmental needs.

Merck strengthened the link to pay by applying consistent standards to determine the achievement level for objectives and by training managers to differentiate performance against the objectives and expectations. The net effect was that more-confident managers held more open, candid discussions around performance assessment, the link to pay, and pay opportunities at the associate level.

The Results

The results of these major change efforts at Merck were measured by its Performance Management Process (PMP) survey, which sampled more than 3,600 associates who had experienced a full performance cycle under the new system. These findings were compared with the results of the 2000 Worldwide Employee Opinion Survey (WEOS), which targeted the entire company population (see Figure 9.1). Merck also made extensive use of focus groups (more than 1,000 associates participated) and conducted a compensation analysis that included more than 17,000 associates.

Figure 9.1: Significant Improvements in Merck's Performance Management System

Favorable Item Comparison	2000 WEOS Merck	2003 PMP Merck	Percentage Point Change
New employees given clear idea of job expectations	60%	74%	+14
Clear idea of my job responsibilities	90%	93%	+3
Supervisor gives regular performance feedback	62%	73%	+11
Last performance review helped identify strengths and weaknesses	44%	60%	+16
Understand my job performance evaluation	67%	84%	+17
My job performance evaluated fairly	64%	81%	+17
Company matches pay to performance	24%	41%	+17
Company too lenient with poor performers*	28%	26%	-2
Company too slow to reward strong performers*	29%	28%	-1

* Reverse-scored item
• 2000 WEOS had an 86% (N=54,008) response rate and was targeted toward the *entire company population*.
• 2003 PMP survey had a 63% (N=3,789) response rate and was targeted toward a *sample* of individuals who experienced the 2002–2003 performance management cycle.

According to Dr. Ross, there are still areas for improvement as Merck manages the process to achieve its original objectives. Two of these include establishing more differentiation in the compensation process and further building managers' skills in giving feedback. However, given the rigor of both the process and the measurement, coupled with the strong senior-level support for the process, the chances for success are good.

At BT Exact, the CEO's realization goal was to raise the performance bar for the 6,000-person operation. As you'll see in reading the following case study, the company achieved that goal.

case study

BT EXACT

BT Exact is British Telecommunication's research, technology, and IT operations business. In 2002 Chief Executive Officer Stewart Davies decided to "raise the performance bar" for his 6,000-person division. He wanted all associates to understand what was expected of them, to have quantifiable objectives, and to know how they were going to meet those expectations. He also wanted each person to see how his or her performance was directly linked to rewards. To achieve all this, Davies was looking for "a vehicle to concentrate employees' minds on clear and specific expectations and the resulting rewards." The vehicle he turned to was performance management.

To ensure that everyone knew that his or her boss was squarely on board and that all managers were fully knowledgeable about the system, all senior executives were trained in a full-day session; all other managers were trained during a two-day session. The senior executives attended a second session one year later to review the progress toward the program goals and to assess feedback from associates on surveys and other feedback loops established on the positive and negative aspects of the program. The senior team then adjusted the system for the second year. Davies even went to the people who suggested improvements and talked to them directly.

These efforts paid off. After the first full year of implementation, BT Exact exceeded its expectations and received more bonuses and rewards than expected. Not surprisingly, this produced immeasurable buy-in to the system. Each month Davies posts the company and division results on the division's web site so that everyone can see how they are doing compared to plan and, consequently, compared to their bonus system.

The Results

After the second full year, Davies feels that BT Exact has, indeed, met his goal for raising the performance bar and that performance management has become a way of life at his organization. Davies believes that roles are clearer and expectations are very apparent. The system, called Maximizing My Performance, is now an imperative that everyone at BT participates in and follows. Davies also commented that the system was a great vehicle for driving the revised set of values.

The Bottom Line

If your organization takes the time and invests the effort required to rigorously address each of these five fundamental implementation components, it will greatly enhance the effectiveness of its performance management system. Will it take a lot of effort? Absolutely. Is it worth the effort? You bet it is. Performance management is a system that affects everyone in the organization. It helps the organization achieve desired business results and maintain its desired culture. It lets associates understand how they are contributing to the organization's goals, what's expected of them, how they are doing, and how they can continue to grow, develop, and add value to the business.

A Deeper Look

While we don't want you to get bogged down in details, we do want you to have an idea of the issues that should be addressed in the course of an implementation. The following outline reflects the logic for the process we employ in our consulting practice.

Performance Management Planning and Schedule

When will the following key events occur?

- Performance Management Planning Meeting
  - Who will champion this effort?
  - Is a team set up to oversee the implementation? Who is on the team? What are their roles? Who is going to make sure they all have an appropriate orientation?
  - Who will provide the necessary resources?
  - When can you kick it off?

- Data Gathering and System Evaluation
  - Assess your existing system. Is it fundamentally flawed? In need of tweaking? Is the system fine, but in need of re-implementation?
  - If it needs substantial redevelopment, what will your model be? Who will redesign it? Should you create or buy? Do you want to speak with a consultant?
  - Will you need custom material development?

- Training
  - Executive training
  - Facilitator selection and training
  - Manager/Leader training
  - Associate training

Expectations

What results are expected from implementing this system? (This is not a question to be taken lightly.) Are you looking to use this system to manage your organization's performance? Will you use it to:

- Communicate and cascade strategic business objectives throughout the organization?

- Communicate and cascade cultural development objectives?

- Serve as the foundation for developing career plans for every associate?

- Drive individual accountability and responsibility?

- Feed other systems (such as compensation, succession planning, training, etc.)?

How receptive is the organization expected to be toward this system by:
- Organizational level?
- Functional area?
- Geographic area?

Degree of Change

Describe the current performance management system components:
- Key result areas
- Development plans
- Objectives
- Interim reviews
- Competencies
- Final review

Define the performance management process:

- Compared with the current system, what will associates see different about this system?
- Any process differences?
- Will administrative practices or policies change?
- Who gets a copy of the performance plan and performance review? How long is this documentation kept? Who has access and for what purposes?

Links to Business Planning

- How will the performance management process fit and support the business planning cycle?
- What is the business planning cycle? Fiscal year? Performance review year? How would you describe the current business planning process in terms of major steps in the cycle and timing? Who is involved in the process? What happens with the output when plans are complete?
- Is information from business planning shared? At what levels? Are there mechanisms in place to ensure the information is shared?
- Links to business planning elements: Are there mechanisms in place to ensure the information is shared (that is, vision, strategic priorities, department or functional goals, values, other)?

Links to Organizational Systems

- How will this system integrate with other organizational systems (such as compensation, selection and promotion, succession planning, executive succession management, career development, assessment, training, rewards and recognition, individual or group development)?
- Are there any conflicts or inconsistencies among these systems?

Legal Defensibility

- Does your corporate counsel need to examine the proposed system?
- Does counsel feel the proposed system adequately provides:
  - Clear expectations?
  - Accurate documentation?
  - Regular performance discussions?
  - Feedback skills?
  - Decisions consistent with performance data?
  - Opportunity for associate comments?
  - Performance management training?

Corporate Self-Defense: The Legal Aspects of Performance Management

How many times have you read about a wrongful dismissal costing a company millions of dollars? With the litigious mind-set so prevalent today, organizations need to ensure that their performance management system can meet the test of legal defensibility.

In cases involving performance data, courts usually ask the employer to provide performance appraisal information and other supporting evidence for the HR decision in question. The main focus of the lawsuit becomes the employer's practice and intent with regard to performance management.

Four personnel actions typically trigger legal action: demotion, failure to promote, layoff, and termination. To place themselves in the strongest possible legal position, organizations need to follow a few critical performance management practices. They need to ensure that:

1. **The performance management system is based on clear, relevant performance objectives and expectations.** Performance goals and objectives (the *whats* in a performance plan) should meet the following criteria: specific, measurable (quantity, quality, cost, timeliness), attainable, relevant, and time bound. Competencies, which are also included in many performance plans, must be observable, related to objectives, understandable, and aligned with the organization's goals and values.

2. **People know the performance objectives and expectations at the start of the performance cycle.** Not only should the objectives and expectations be clear and meet the criteria above, but they also must be communicated to and understood by associates.

3. **Interim and final reviews accurately and specifically reflect performance.** The more performance is discussed and the more open and candid the discussions are, the more defensible the system is. When performance issues go undiscussed or unreported, the door is left open to legal action by the associate. Continuous feedback throughout the performance cycle is a necessity, with the summary discussion being documented.

4. **People receive a written performance review at least once a year.** At the end of the performance cycle, there must be a discussion that summarizes an associate's performance for that year. The manager obviously has the final say in whatever rating process the organization uses, but the more involvement the associate has in the process, the less the likelihood of legal issues down the road.

5. **Associates have an opportunity to comment on the performance review.** If there is disagreement on performance levels, the associate has a right to document that disagreement or any other comments relevant to his or her performance. If major differences are evident, the organization should attempt to resolve them, if possible.

6. **Managers are trained in all aspects of the system.** There are many critical tasks/activities involved in efficiently managing associates' performance. Many of them involve using skills that simply don't come under the title of *manager*. Few things impress the court more than documentation that shows an organization has provided managers with comprehensive training covering all major aspects of the performance management process, including:

- Setting performance objectives and expectations.
- Gaining agreement on performance objectives and expectations.
- Tracking performance and providing feedback.
- Coaching.
- Evaluating performance levels.
- Conducting performance review discussions.

CHAPTER 10

THE ROLE OF TECHNOLOGY

Chapter Overview

The role of technology in any field—including performance management—is to make a given task go more quickly or become easier, more efficient, or more convenient than it is without the technology. The paper forms we use are one level of technology. For the purposes of this discussion, however, we will examine two higher forms of technological support.

Training people to use a performance management system is a very expensive proposition, particularly so if an organization's workforce is distributed around the globe. Technology, in the form of CD-ROM-based instruction, "webinars" (that is, training sessions conducted via the Internet or a company's intranet), or 100 percent web-delivered training, can sometimes be adequately effective and cost considerably less than traditional classroom instruction.

There are very few systems in any organization's universe not affected by technology. For some reason, however, performance management systems seem to be among the last systems to be brought online. The justification for this probably relates to the value most organizations place on performance management as a serious tool for executing strategic objectives. After all, if performance management is perceived as a *pro forma* annual ritual, why would top management care about investing in IT for it? On the other hand, if the CEO is serious about letting associates track their own performance, serious about linking performance management with other systems (compensation, recruitment, on-boarding, training, etc.), and serious about making it easy for everyone (managers and associates alike) to access the information, then of course it would go online.

This chapter will look at a few examples of how technology has worked effectively to make a real difference for companies who are serious about getting the most out of their performance management systems.

What to Expect from Technology

Performance management software is *supposed* to streamline the evaluation process, reduce paperwork, encourage objectivity, facilitate the sharing of information between functions, and make it easier for leaders and associates to contribute and access data in the system.

That is how it's *supposed* to work. Sometimes, it does; sometimes, it doesn't. Either way, it costs a hefty sum. And if technology does not yield the desired results, there will be one of two reasons why: 1) the technology is simply automating a bad process, or 2) the system was not fitted well to the organization. In the former case, we refer you to the preceding chapters and advise your organization to decide exactly how you want the system to work and be used (starting with the executive suite and line managers) before you get too concerned with an IT solution.

In the case of a poor fit, we encourage your organization to be very cautious in its system selection and with the people doing the training and implementation. Given that the system is effective and making a substantial contribution to your organization's ability to execute its strategic objectives, your prime concern should be fitting the software to your system. A software package that cannot be customized to your needs is a software system that you don't need.

So, what should you expect from a software solution?

Real-Time Access

For starters, you can expect real-time access to your performance management system. That means everyone—leaders and associates—can contribute data to the system or read data from it as needed. It means that, rather than completing a pen-and-paper form and waiting for it to creep across a series of desks over a period of weeks and requiring much labor-intensive handling, a screen or two can be filled out and instantly be made available wherever the data is needed. And neither time nor geography is relevant. An employee in Helsinki can submit a performance appraisal to HR at corporate headquarters in Silicon Valley at 1 p.m. PST more easily than if the person put a form in interoffice mail downstairs. Pretty cool stuff, is it not?

But the advantage of an online performance management system reflects much more than the capability to fill out a form more easily. If an organization has made the transformation to an online system, the real-time opportunity for managing work and performance is compounded exponentially. Imagine associates in 10 geographically dispersed locations of a global organization working on a critical initiative that supports a key strategic priority. In one of the better software systems, progress can be tracked regularly through status updates generated on key objectives of individuals or leaders in the system. If three or four locations are struggling with a particular initiative, that trend can be observed and detected far earlier than without such a system. Likewise, if all 10 are observed to be on track, think of the relief for senior executives who have a lot riding on the success of the initiative.

Perceived Greater Objectivity

Another frequently reported advantage of online systems is that associates perceive them as being more objective and open. More objective because software-based appraisals tend to focus more on results and actions than on personality traits. More open because associates can see their performance evaluations and track progress toward their goals. This allows them to make strategic changes to improve their progress, question comments, and correct mistakes in documentation.

Automatic Alignment

As we explained in Chapter 2 on strategy execution, a performance management system that aligns the CEO's objectives (that is, the organization's strategic priorities) with each subsequent level of leadership—down to the frontline employees—significantly increases the probability of its success. An online performance management system makes this process much, much easier. An effective software system forces objectives to align with a higher-level objective—all the way to the top of the organization.

We frequently review the alignment and accomplishment of key objectives at various levels in DDI to ensure that progress is on track and that people are working on the key priorities for our company. By having that information at a senior leader's fingertips, an organization can ensure that people are working on the right things and that the activities being done, reviewed, coached, and evaluated are those that will have the greatest impact on bottom-line results. This also makes work more meaningful for associates, and boosts their feelings of partnership, commitment, and overall engagement in their jobs. What more could we want?

Performance Tracking Made Easier

Over the years our work in performance management has helped us identify the best practices for success. One of the most crucial best practices is getting leaders and associates to discuss performance on an ongoing basis— not just once or twice a year. A technologically based system that provides for ongoing tracking of performance and, therefore, the likelihood of more frequent, informal discussions around performance, can inspire more frequent coaching sessions, reinforcement meetings, and mid-course adjustments. Similarly, if associates and leaders are tracking performance in real time, the summary review will cover the entire period of performance—not just the data collected most recently (as is often the case in a paper-based system).

Standardizing the system as democratically and impartially as only computer software can also tends to ensure that leaders and their direct reports address the developmental components in their performance plans.

Easy Access to Data

Yet another substantial benefit of an online system is the visibility of the data and the ease of generating reports. Because the data resides in one place, if the organization so chooses, information can be shared on the progress and status of linked key initiatives. This visibility can help associates in their own jobs by increasing their understanding of how their particular role fits into the big picture, expanding their partnership opportunities, and reducing redundancy and conflict. What's more, because the technology is still so new, there are many additional benefits yet to be discovered. Reports that are available in most systems can be great tools not only for summary reviews and evaluations, but also—and more meaningfully—as discussion points for coaching, mentoring sessions, or as backup information when more difficult intervention discussions are necessary.

No Substitute for Human Interactions

When we talk with people about an online system, one of their greatest concerns is that a technology-facilitated system will eliminate the interactions needed for performance management to be effective. No matter what its advantages, technology will never substitute for necessary human interactions. We understand that some other automated systems that monitor boundaries, variances, etc., for things such as safety, chemical mix, or tolerance levels might lull people into a false sense of security. That should not be allowed to happen in a performance management system. Performance management technology is meant to be an enabler, not a replacement. However, an online system can and should reduce the time people need for interactions and identify the data or results that will best focus the efforts of these interactions. This is an incredibly positive effect and aligns perfectly with the best practices we've observed.

Before you throw a software system into the works, consider the communication and training homework you'll need to do to ensure its success. Even if your existing non-computerized performance management system is working flawlessly, you'll need to make sure that your workforce understands the need for change and has the skills to make the change work and that the whole shebang has the support of line management.

Technology and Training

Technology can empower a performance management system in other ways too. In addition to putting the system online, the most common application is training. There are quite a few benefits an organization might enjoy by conducting training either through a distance-learning or computer-assisted mode:

- **Cost savings.** Travel expenses are reduced or eliminated.

- **Continued productivity.** Because associates need not leave the workplace for extended periods, there is minimal disruption to productivity.

- **Real-time results.** Our experience in 30 years of training has taught us that "teachable moments" are the best time for training. When the need is real time (now!), more learning occurs because of its immediate applicability.

- **Learning anytime.** Computer-assisted learning can be delivered whenever associates want or need it.

- **Consistent approach.** Geographically dispersed groups can receive the same training anywhere in the world.

Lockheed Martin represents an excellent example of how a large corporate entity (125,000 associates) leveraged technology to implement a web-based version of its performance management system. And it trained most of its associates in a single day!

case study

LOCKHEED MARTIN

Lockheed Martin is a consolidation of 17 companies, many of which are advanced technology and defense based. In 1999 Lockheed undertook a far-reaching best practices initiative to foster a "One Company/One Team" philosophy for the 125,000 associates in its global workforce.

In conjunction with this initiative, Lockheed developed the Performance Recognition System (PRS) in 2000 and began installing it that same year. The PRS had several ambitious objectives:

- Align associate objectives with organizational goals.

- Instill organizational values and standards.

- Provide feedback to let associates know how they're doing.

- Support professional development.

- Provide information to help determine merit salary increases, promotions, and other recognition.

The organization began implementing a web-based version of PRS in 2002, rolling it out to 36,000 associates; by the end of 2003, more than 71,000 associates were using the system via computer networks.

To guarantee that its entire workforce was "singing from the same song sheet," Lockheed trained most of its associates in a full-day session at the start of the rollout.

The process Lockheed selected included the following notable components:

1. Goals and objectives are set at the beginning of the year after having been carefully aligned to business unit goals, which are posted online so that everybody can see the same clear set of objectives.

2. Each associate initiates an online self-assessment and a multirater process, with the person and his or her manager agreeing on raters.

3. Once multirater surveys are completed, the manager writes a performance summary and schedules a meeting with the associate.

4. During the meeting they discuss and agree on a final assessment and ratings.

5. All major documents are hosted online, and the associate acknowledges completing the cycle.

The rating system includes an overall rating used with distribution guidelines. It's important to note that the ratings are assigned with guidelines and are not forced. The ratings are, however, monitored for alignment with the guidelines. Lockheed Martin's performance management system incorporates the following ratings and distribution guidelines:

Table 10.1: Rating Distribution Guidelines

Rating	Guideline
Exceptional	0–15%
High contributor	10–25%
Successful contributor	40–70%
Basic contributor	0–15%
Unsatisfactory	0–3%

The Results

Lockheed has been quite pleased with the results.

- Associates' objectives are linked more directly than ever to business unit goals and strategies. A 2003 survey showed that 130 percent more associates (than in 2001) see a clear link between their work and the company's objectives.

- The quality of feedback associates received showed a 14 percent improvement as reflected in their responses to this survey item: "I received ongoing feedback that helps me improve my performance."

One perk of the online system is that it has forced more compliance. If an associate has not completed his or her part of the data collection, the information to initiate a pay increase is not there. No data, no raise. While this has generated some complaints, it also has increased compliance to the system.

In 2003 Lockheed Martin completed 96 percent of all performance reviews by its stated deadline and 99 percent within one week of the deadline. The online system had an amazing 862,520 visits during the year and more than 91 million hits. The average number of visits per day exceeded 8,000. The system now has become a way of life at Lockheed Martin.

CHAPTER 11

DO YOU NEED A CONSULTANT?

Chapter Overview

I fretted a bit about writing this chapter. Here we are, clearly in the business of consulting with clients regarding their performance management systems. How can we expect to be objective or to expect you to perceive us as being objective?

Well, we can't.

And, honestly, we're not objective. In fact, we're highly biased. We believe, based on the preponderance of survey data, that most companies are not realizing much benefit from their performance management system. Further, we believe that if those companies could cure themselves, they would have done so long ago. Performance management, although it's hardly an exotic subject, is something that most often is beyond the means of most organizations to repair. There are good reasons for this, and we examine them in this chapter.

So, unless your organization is capable of effecting such a significant change on its own, you should consider getting some help. The extent of help needed can vary widely. This chapter discusses several areas around consulting on performance management:

- What is the benefit of engaging a consultant?
- What is the role of the consultant?
- How do you select a consultant?

The Benefits of Using a Consultant

Consultants can be either an enormous waste of time and money or just the catalyst you need to jump-start your company to begin realizing results. In the arena of performance management, we've seen both kinds of outcomes—including instances when our company's services were used. Even with excellent products and services, if the consultant isn't utilized properly, an organization might be wasting its time and money. So how does your organization decide if it needs a consultant?

Let's say that you're not getting the results you'd like from your performance management system. You have further determined that you are committed to getting a system that delivers the desired results. There are two questions that you must ask yourself:

1. Do you have the in-house skills and resources to overhaul your system?

2. If so, do these people have the time to accomplish the task?

If the answer to either question is no, you'll probably need to use consultants. You might use them to assess your system, determine whether it needs a minor tweaking and proper implementation (versus a ground-to-top reengineering), design a new system, or lead your team through each step of an implementation.

The benefits of engaging a consultant with years of experience in performance management can be significant. These people have seen what works and what doesn't. Installing a performance management system is not about the basics of instituting a new form or training people to use the system. Instead, it's more about facilitating the change process itself and doing what it takes to achieve realization (that is, formulating the communication strategy, figuring out how to drive accountability for the new system, knowing what not to do on the compensation side, and determining how to measure the effectiveness of the system).

Role of the Consultant

Consultants can play one of four roles for an organization:

- **Expert.** Consultants with the right expertise and experience can provide best-practice techniques that increase the likelihood of success. They have answers for each step in the process based on their experience. You should listen to them.

- **Facilitator.** Some senior line managers don't like to be "told." Rather, they prefer that an outside consultant pull the right ideas or practices from the experience in the group. One CEO of a hotel chain once told us, "Whatever you do, don't ever mention what our chief competitor does—we don't want to hear it." In these situations the consultant steers the group in the right direction through questions and the experience of the senior team's members. Some consultants who are experts have difficulty with this role.

- **Pair of hands.** At times an organization might need a consultant simply as another resource to get something done. In these cases the decision of what and how has already been made; the organization just needs another pair of hands to complete the task. While most consultants don't want to perform in this role (and, frankly, it's usually a waste of a valuable resource), some organizations feel the need to use consultants in this way. We know of a large pharmaceutical company that had its compensation committee drive the performance management system. The new system had already been developed, and top management wanted a consultant to deliver the training. When we informed them of the flaws we saw in their system (never let the compensation committee be the final decision makers on a performance management system), they didn't want to change and gave the training contract to someone else. Obviously, they just wanted a pair of hands—not someone who would improve their system based on an extensive history of working with many different systems.

- **Partner.** Here, the consultant plays a variety of roles. At times an expert, at times a pair of hands, at times a facilitator—but always working to do what's best for the client. Partner consultants still use experience and expertise to guide their clients toward success. They have the best interests of the client at heart because they know the client will (most likely) reward them with future business. Partner consultants cultivate levels of trust and communication commensurate with being a true partner. Now this sounds like the role a consultant should always play—but it doesn't work out that way in many instances. Some organizations like to keep consultants more at an arm's length for fear they will learn too much and somehow take advantage of the situation. Some simply prefer not to be as honest with an outsider as is required to cultivate the openness and trust needed to forge a true partnership.

Whatever role you want an outside consultant to play, it's very important to gain agreement up front on what that role is. Depending on the in-house expertise available, the view senior management has of outside consultants, and the likelihood for multiple projects with the consultants, you can decide which role or roles you want the consultant to play.

The "Challenger"

With performance management projects, there is another potential role an outside consultant can play: "challenger." This role may be a subset of the "expert" or "partner" roles, but requires the consultant to really challenge the senior executives to do what's necessary to drive the performance management system. We've already shown the need for senior executives— particularly, the CEO—to champion the system, but it might take an outsider to push these leaders to do the things that will make the difference. For example, will they use the system with their subordinate senior leaders? Will they drive and monitor the completion of the process with quality and consistency? Will they push the accountabilities linked to the strategic priorities down through the organization? Will they take action with senior leaders who don't use the system correctly?

Senior executives who won't take on these tasks are exercising what we call a silent veto. In performance management there is no middle ground—you are either an articulate advocate of the system (meaning you are passionate and willing to communicate your passion about the value of performance management), or you are silent, which communicates to everyone that you are not positive. Senior executives who remain silent aren't helping to make the system work better and be sustainable over time.

How Do You Select a Consultant?

Consultants vary greatly in their level of expertise, and they lose much value when they get out of their area of proficiency. When selecting a consultant to help revamp your organization's performance management system, it's helpful to get answers to these three questions:

- **What is the consultant's special area of expertise?** Does the consultant's skill set match what you want him or her to do for you? In this instance you are looking for very specific expertise. The consultant you choose should have a great deal of experience with performance management systems—period. Ask if the consultant has done similar work for other organizations of similar size, industry, culture, etc. There might be exceptions to this guideline in other areas, but not in performance management.

- **What is the consultant's view of performance management?** If, after reading this book, you are certain that your performance management system is going to be a significant management tool for executing your strategic objectives, your consultant better perceive it in the same way. You'll want a consultant who specializes in implementing performance management systems that work—for years. Get references. Take care to make sure that the person will be credible with your senior executives.

- **Does the consultant have experience in using the system?** There are few consultants who practice all that they preach. This can lead to impractical solutions and advice if the consultant is advocating logical, but complex, theories that will not work as well as they sound. The two most difficult HR systems to get right are compensation and performance management. Use a consultant who not only understands the theory, but who also has experience in personally implementing a particular system.

The Consultant's References

Although references are a valuable tool when selecting a consultant, they often are overlooked or ignored. Here are some guidelines for obtaining and using references wisely.

- **Ask for references.** Specifically ask what the consultant did for the organization used as a reference. Was the work the same as the work you want the person to do for you? If it matches, the reference can provide you valuable information about the consultant's work. If it doesn't, the reference might be of limited value to you.

- **Ask the reference if he or she was satisfied with the consultant's work.** If not, why? If possible, ask for a copy of the report the consultant wrote for the reference.

- **Ask the reference in-depth questions about the consultant's work.** This might trigger memories of problems or concerns the reference might have experienced with the consultant.

- **Check more than one or two references.**

- **Research the consultant's track record.** How long is the person's client list? For the long term, a consultant's most valuable asset is a list of satisfied clients. In today's business environment there are many early retirees, along with many others rendered jobless due to corporate downsizing, who have begun to work as independent consultants. Check with their former employers and others in the industry.

EPILOGUE: THE DREAM

The Promise of Performance Management Realized

Boldcase International is truly an amazing company and one of the best places for people to work. A highly successful consumer products company, Boldcase has surpassed the average growth rate in its industry for 10 consecutive years. It is now seen as the number two company in its field. What makes Boldcase so successful is a combination of a clear strategic direction and a culture that makes associates feel valued and motivated to make the company better each day. Boldcase wasn't always this successful, but in 1993 a new CEO turned things around in a big way.

After a few months of diagnosing what was needed, the CEO undertook a number of initiatives that led Boldcase to the astonishing results it has achieved. The first thing she did was institute a balanced scorecard that focused on the customer, process, and people strategies to produce better financial results. Once the senior team agreed on the key areas of focus, the CEO implemented an aggressive accountability system that aligned the senior team's performance accountabilities with those in the balanced scorecard. She also redefined the culture strategy for the organization to better align it with the customer focus she emphasized in the scorecard measures.

Once the senior team's accountabilities were clear for the business and cultural strategies, the CEO used an online performance management system to align all associate goals to the senior team's goals. This align-ment generated a stream of energy and passion on the same key factors that determined the business success. The performance management system also focused on the key competencies and behaviors that would drive a customer-first culture and that would sharpen the focus on customer satisfaction and retention. The CEO instituted biannual reviews and promoted much greater associate ownership of the system, which relieved management of some tedious work associated with the system. Associates quickly saw the benefits of this change, willingly accepted their new roles in this system, and implemented it with a true sense of empowerment.

Amazingly, upward communications dramatically improved on the key issues measured in the balanced scorecard. Retention improved as company performance began to climb, and Boldcase quickly became an employer of choice as people flocked to become part of a winning organization.

APPENDIX
THE SYSTEM: NUTS AND BOLTS

I don't want to belabor you with a thorough discussion of exactly how a well-implemented performance management system works. There are textbooks, consultants, and training programs galore that can fulfill that mission.

But I do want to give you enough of an overview that you can take a look at your system and make sure that it has the necessary nuts and bolts in place to work.

Remember, a system with all the necessary hardware in place does not guarantee all the results that are possible—only that the system is available to be realized. I hearken back to the dairy cow metaphor: Going through all the trouble of keeping a cow well fed and in good health does not put milk and cheese on your table. Your organization must 1) understand the value of the performance management process and the data it provides, and 2) take advantage of these outputs.

The system I describe comprises a familiar three-phase process: Planning, Performing, and Reviewing. I'll take you through each step, show you the forms we use, and describe the nature of the interactions along the way.

Your role, after reading this, is to ensure that the pieces to make the performance management system work are in place and, if they are not already, to get that process moving.

What the Process Looks Like

A performance management system should be designed to ensure that all associates:

- Know what is expected of them.
- Have a performance plan that they had a part in defining and for which they track their own progress.
- Have a say in their evaluations.

- Receive a personal development plan tailored to their particular skill requirements and future career development plans.

- Understand the goals of the whole organization and how their performance is related to these goals and even a great deal more.

In addition, a performance management system should be designed to ensure that the organization achieves alignment and accountability in realizing its strategic and cultural objectives.

Let's go back to our diagram about driving accountability (Figure A.1):

Figure A.1: Driving Accountability

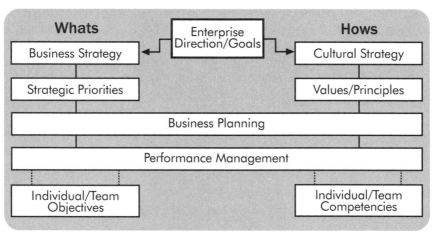

We said that the column on the left describes the *whats* involved with achieving your organization's vision or mission, and that the column on the right includes the *hows* (or the means by which the whats can be accomplished). As you read on, you'll notice that the entire process—all three phases—follows this model, integrating strategic and cultural objectives into a plan for each associate across the entire organization.

Introduction to the Planning Phase

The Planning phase includes three components:

- A listing of the results (that is, key result areas and objectives) each associate needs to achieve.

- A listing of the knowledge, skills, and behaviors (also known as competencies) needed by each associate to achieve those results.

- A development plan listing activities that will help each associate grow in his or her job or attain the skills needed for a new job.

Keep in mind that each component needs to be linked to the organization's vision, values, and strategic priorities. All the following presupposes that training has already been provided or that training is being offered concurrently with the implementation. With that in mind, to ensure the Planning phase works as effectively as it should, we recommend the following:

1. Provide associates at each level with the 1) organizationwide and departmental or functional area's goals, 2) organizational vision and values, and 3) strategic priorities. Each associate also must consider his or her individual desires for development, given the data provided about the needs of the organization and the person's department or functional area.

2. It is then up to each associate to consider that data in light of his or her job and to formulate 1) key result areas, objectives, and measurement criteria; 2) competencies; and 3) a development plan for acquiring skills that will advance the associate in his or her chosen direction.

3. Each associate then brings a tentative plan to his or her leader in an individual meeting we call a reaching agreement discussion. The result of that meeting is an agreed-upon performance plan that the associate will be responsible for tracking.

Introduction to the Performing Phase

The Performing phase is the longest of the three phases and fills the period between Planning and Reviewing—generally a year of work. During this period each associate is responsible for tracking his or her own performance.

Managers are responsible for providing ongoing feedback and coaching. In some implementations coworkers and customers also can provide feedback about an associate's strengths and opportunities for improvement.

Interim discussions, which can be either formally scheduled or impromptu meetings, also should be held to make sure the objectives set during the Planning phase are being met. Ongoing monitoring and joint problem-solving efforts ensure that problems are corrected as they arise and that modifications to the plan can be made before it's too late to respond constructively.

Introduction to the Reviewing Phase

Associates and their managers meet at the end of the Performing phase to discuss accomplishments and contributions and, in general, to agree on performance ratings. This discussion answers the associate's question,

"How have I done?" with input from both parties. This discussion should include:

- A summary of all the interim discussions held up to that point, including a look at any new data collected since the last meeting.

- A review of how the associate's actual results measured up to the initial plan. There should be no surprises here if both parties have been regularly communicating during the Performing phase.

- An opportunity to decide what can be done to improve and develop in the future.

The Form

As long as we are revealing the inner workings of the black box, we will share the basic form we use, at least as a starting point, for performance management. Figure A.2 is a sample form condensed to one page from several pages for ease of use in this book. We'll fill in this form as we describe the process on the following pages.

Sample Performance Worksheet

Name:

Job/Role:

Performance Cycle:

Reaching Agreement Date:

Part I: The Whats

Key Result Areas	Objectives	Tracking Sources	Actual Results	Ratings

Part II: The Hows

Competencies	Key Actions	Tracking Sources	Actual Results (STARs)	Ratings

Part III: Development Plan

LEARNING NEED		Developmental Activities	By When
Competencies	Key Actions		

Phase One: Planning

The Performance Worksheet we recommend is made up of three parts:

1. The whats (strategic objectives)
2. The hows (cultural objectives)
3. The development plan (individual and career development)

We recommend that the organization make each associate responsible for participating fully in the Planning phase. To do this, you need to provide people with data about what the organization expects to achieve (strategic and cultural objectives) and how that is being broken down into their departmental or functional area's goals. Each associate then needs to think about his or her job in terms of the results he or she is responsible for delivering. A great many associates do not have a very clear grasp of this.

Key Result Areas

The first component of the performance plan deals with the individual's share of the organization's strategic objectives. One way for associates to become clearer about the outputs of their jobs—and the method we advocate—is for them to develop their key result areas. KRAs are the reason a job exists. They are broad categories expressed as general outputs or outcomes. For example, a KRA for an information systems analyst might be software maintenance; for someone in a manufacturing setting, safety.

KRAs should:

- Support the department's or functional area's goals.
- Number between three and seven.
- Be described in a few words that don't indicate how much or by when.
- Be within the influence of the associate.
- Not change unless the job changes.

Examples of KRAs include customer satisfaction, departmental support, expense management, and training and development.

Objectives

Objectives are the specific tasks a person needs to perform and the results he or she needs to achieve in the key result areas. Clearly written, specific objectives:

- Give each associate clear accountabilities. Associates will know what's expected, and during the year they will know how their results measure up to those expectations.
- Enable associates to more easily track and document performance.

- Help to ensure that jobs are more meaningful and manageable.
- Support the goals of the department or functional area and those of the organization.
- Number from one to three per KRA.

Objectives should be written with the following characteristics in mind. (We have arranged these characteristics into an acronym, "SMART," to make them easier to remember.)

- **Specific.** Objectives should be written in specific terms to avoid confusion about what is to occur or what is to improve. They define results to be accomplished within the scope of the job (for example, "Achieve an average call quota of . . ." or "Respond to all customer requests . . .").

- **Measurable.** Defining measurements for objectives is important for enabling you and the associate to determine and measure results. A measurable objective defines quantity, cost, or quality.

- **Attainable.** Objectives should be challenging, yet attainable.

- **Relevant.** Objectives should be understood in the context of how that work fits into the workings of the department or functional area and the organization as a whole.

- **Time bound.** Objectives must be time bound. Deadlines or frequency of occurrence must be stipulated.

Tracking Progress

Associates track their progress through a variety of sources, including reports, surveys, internal interview data, evaluations, quality specifications, time logs, complaint logs, manager observations, audit results, certificates of completion, etc.

Involving associates in selecting measures and performance scorecards will revolutionize measurement in any organization that dares to give them a try. Here are some ideas for generating excitement about measurement:

- Educate associates about measurement. Sponsor educational programs centering on work measurement.

- Have senior managers visit areas of the company that are involved in innovative measurement activities to offer encouragement and support.

- Talk to associates about measurement whenever you get a chance. Ask them about the measures they are using. Show a personal interest in their work and how it's measured.

- Sponsor kick-off celebrations for new measurement initiatives with appropriate fanfare and ceremony.

- Recognize associates' contributions to measurement activities. Feedback is the vehicle for communicating performance measurement data. Although measurement data provides some built-in feedback, few of us are able to adjust our performance based on measurement data alone.

How KRAs, Objectives, and Tracking Fit Together

At this point in the cycle, each associate has reviewed the organizational and the departmental or functional area's strategic objectives and cultural or value objectives. The associate has evaluated his or her job and identified three to seven KRAs that define the main reasons for the job's existence. Within each of those KRAs, the associate also has identified several objectives that serve to translate that broad area into specific, measurable items. Here are a few examples of how objectives might fit into the KRAs:

Figure A.3: Sample Performance Worksheet—the Whats

Key Result Areas	Objectives	Tracking Sources	Actual Results	Ratings
Customer Satisfaction	• Achieve an average call quota of 70 calls per day.	• Statistical reports		
	• Respond to all customer requests within 24 hours.	• Problem tracking sheets		
	• Receive an average minimum rating of 3 on a 5-point scale in each quarterly customer satisfaction audit.	• Audit results		
Department Support	• Provide phone coverage during breaks, lunches, and vacations according to weekly assignments.	• Self-report and team feedback		
Expense Management	• Do not exceed $500 a month in customer recovery payments without prior authorization	• Budget reports		
Training and Development	• Complete training in XYZ by October 31.	• Training certificate		

How Many Objectives?

Usually, one to three objectives per KRA are sufficient to ensure that associates are doing their part toward the organizationwide accomplishment of a strategic objective. With three to seven KRAs, this would suggest that each associate might have as many as 21 objectives, but 10 to 15 are ideal. More than 15 objectives generally indicates an associate has too many important results to focus on.

Competencies

The second component of the performance plan pertains to competencies, which are the hows of performance—the knowledge, motivation, and behaviors people display to achieve results. Competencies uphold the organization's values. They represent the way people define and live the values. A few examples of competencies are Customer Focus, Planning and Organizing, and Technical/Professional Knowledge and Skills.

Although they vary by job, competencies affect associates' ability to achieve results. They also determine the climate of any given organization. The process of realizing a competency is accomplished in much the same way as with strategic objectives. We suggest that each associate select between one and three competency areas on which to work for each performance cycle.

Reporting results on competency development might best be accomplished by recording behavioral examples that describe how a person used a competency in a specific situation to achieve a specific result. We call these behavioral examples STARs (Situation or Task, Action, and Result), and they can provide a valuable snapshot of how an associate exhibited a competency in a certain context.

Using our form, the competency portion of the performance plan might look like this:

Figure A.4: Sample Performance Worksheet—the Hows

Competencies	Key Actions	Tracking Sources	Actual Results (STARs)	Ratings
Customer Focus	• Follows up with customers. • Takes responsibility for handling specific customer problems or requests.	Customer comments, self-report, leader and team feedback		
Planning and Organizing	• Establishes priorities. • Sequences activities.	Problem tracking sheets, customer comments, self-report, team feedback		
Technical/ Professional Knowledge and Skills	• Attends training courses on current developments. • Uses knowledge of facilities, capabilities, and capacities to achieve tasks and solve problems.	Self-report, training certificates, and leader and team feedback		

Development Plans

Basic competency development is one thing; the long-term development needs of an individual are another. That is where the third component of the performance plan—the development plan—comes into play. Previous chapters have discussed how developing associates can be instrumental to an organization's retention efforts. Here is how a development plan might look:

Figure A.5: Sample Performance Worksheet—Development Plan

LEARNING NEED		Developmental Activities	By When
Competencies	Key Actions		
Technical Proficiency	• Attends training courses on current developments. • Uses knowledge of facilities, capabilities, and capacities to achieve tasks and solve problems.	• Complete advanced training in XYZ before end of performance cycle. • Complete interaction skills training before end of next performance cycle.	
Planning and Organizing	• Establishes priorities. • Sequences activities.	• Use calendar to set priorities. • Complete time management training by end of second quarter.	

Reaching Agreement Discussion

We strongly recommend that your organization provide associates with the data they'll need and the accountability to complete a draft of their performance plan in advance of their reaching agreement discussion.

The more your organization can support its associates as the driver of this process, the better it will be in terms of associate ownership. Once you have given every associate the game plans for the organization and the department or functional area, you can let each person have a voice in how to best support that direction.

During the reaching agreement discussion, it's the manager's job to act as reviewer and coach for the final version of the performance plan. The purpose of this meeting is for the manager and associate to discuss and agree on objectives the associate has identified for both current and long-term roles and to set priorities for what can realistically be accomplished in the current performance cycle.

Let's face it: Development is difficult. People don't change unless they really work at it. They're more likely to do that work when they feel supported and respected. Managers can have a significant impact on people's willingness to develop new skills and reach higher levels of performance. To create an environment that encourages continuous associate development, managers need to:

- Be sure people know what they need to develop and why. They must help associates diagnose their developmental needs.

- Determine how receptive associates are to development and feedback. Do they look for ways to improve, or do they get defensive?

- Tie development in competencies to the achievement of objectives.

- Encourage associates to pursue developmental activities that suit their styles and motivations.

- Help associates manage their development efforts. This means making sure that they have a vision of how they will accomplish each step and that they are confident and competent before they take off on their own. By providing positive models and setting up people for success, managers can build trust and encourage them to take on future challenges. When people take on too much too quickly, they might fail and shy away from subsequent opportunities to stretch.

- Reinforce incremental and overall improvement in the skill area.

- Monitor progress toward goals and provide coaching and reinforcement when needed.

- Work with associates to identify opportunities to apply their new skills.

- Share some of their own developmental activities. This reinforces the fact that continuous improvement is part of everybody's plan.

Phase Two: Performing

During the Performing phase four things are going on to help keep the plan on track:

- Associates are responsible for tracking their progress according to the agreed-upon tracking sources. Some forms of this documentation will probably require follow-up (see STARs on the following pages).

- Associates are well advised to seek and act on feedback regarding both the whats and hows of their plan.

- Both leaders and associates should be aware of opportunities for coaching and support. There is no better way for a leader to be recognized as supportive than by supporting. Given that the top reason people give for considering leaving their jobs is a less-than-ideal relationship with their leaders, it makes sense that leaders proactively support associates in successfully carrying out their plans.

- Leaders should initiate interim reviews to minimize undesirable surprises. At least once—and it could be a great many more times than that—during the year, managers should schedule a formal interim review to gauge progress.

Once they agree on the associate's performance plan, the leader and associate then have a year to run that plan. In too many organizations the next time the plan is examined is a year later. This is a recipe for disaster. Ideally, the year should include frequent exchanges, initiated by both parties, around the associate's progress with the plan. A few of the more- and less-formal ways of keeping current with a plan include:

- Formal interim reviews of progress with the plan, with problem solving around areas of difficulty.

- Casual conversations initiated by the leader to seek updates on progress.

- Requests for advice or assistance initiated by the associate.

Frequent communication eliminates surprises. The last thing anyone in the organization needs is for people to hold on to problems beyond the point of resolution. Many people prefer to try to save face by not sharing their difficulties; however, the more often communication is initiated, the more likely it will be perceived as helpful and not punitive.

Tracking and STARs

During the Performing phase both the leader and associate should be tracking performance and collecting STARs (remember, these are behavioral examples that describe the Situation or Task, Action, and Result) to document progress toward competency development.

Associates and their managers must remain current with both their tracking and reporting of STARs. Falling behind on reporting is quite easy to do, and it can be quite difficult, amid all the other responsibilities associates have, to catch up. In particular, STARs should be recorded when the information is fresh in mind.

STARs for development of the Customer Focus competency might look like this:

SITUATION #1:

Baynard Industries reported they received the wrong size framises and wanted the situation corrected immediately.

Action: I apologized for the mistake, determined whom to call in Shipping, and arranged for overnight delivery of the right framises. I then called the customer and told them when to expect the shipment. I called the next day to confirm that the framises had arrived.

Result: We recovered from the mistake and resolved the customer problem quickly.

SITUATION #2:

Ned Phillips, from Cravert Industries, called to complain about being rushed off the phone before his problem was resolved.

Action: I called him to apologize and then resolved his problem promptly.

Result: An unhappy customer was satisfied.

ADDITIONAL POSITIVE STARS:

3. Letter from Amalgamated Federated (attached).

4. Letters from two account managers (attached).

Interim Reviews

As we've said, interim reviews during the Performing phase are a very good idea. We have mentioned that top-tier companies like Dell, HCA, GE, and Gillette check on plan progress at least four times a year. During an interim review the associate should be prepared to review performance to date and to have tracking up to date. Any requests to change the plan should be clearly thought out.

It is the associate's responsibility to prepare the leader before the meeting by furnishing the documentation they will review. The leader has the responsibility to read this documentation in advance of the meeting and to be prepared to discuss results to date.

Interim reviews may be scheduled one-quarter or halfway into the performance period, or they can be held after the completion of a major project. It is more important to make sure they occur than to get hung up on how to determine their scheduling.

Phase Three: Reviewing

At the conclusion of the previous performance cycle, the manager and associate agreed on a plan. In the time since, both have tracked progress and have met—both formally and informally—to review that progress. The Reviewing discussion should be no more than a summary of that data. There should be no substantial surprises. In fact, unencumbered by forced rankings or discussions about compensation, this discussion should be the easiest so far.

In preparing for the review, the associate:

1. Gathers and collates available performance data.

2. Makes sure that all results and STARs have been recorded.

3. Determines tentative ratings for each objective and competency.

4. Identifies strengths and development needs.

5. Provides the leader with a copy of the completed performance worksheet.

In preparing for the review, the leader:

1. Reviews the data the associate provides in advance.

2. Gathers additional data he or she wants to present.

3. Evaluates the data and determines tentative ratings.

4. Identifies the associate's strengths and weaknesses.

5. Arranges for a quiet, private place and adequate time to discuss the plan.

As in other discussions, the associate takes the lead in working through this process, while the leader plays a more supportive role. And, as with the reaching agreement discussion, this discussion is simple and straightforward.

The associate:

• Opens by stating purpose and importance.

• Uses his or her completed performance worksheet as a guide to discuss final results, agree on ratings, and identify strengths and areas for improvement.

• Closes by summarizing action steps.

The leader:

• Encourages the associate to lead the discussion.

• Encourages the associate to share performance data and rationale for ratings while asking clarifying questions.

- Shares additional performance data, including STARs collected since the last interim review.
- Discusses the associate's strengths and areas for improvement.

If a leader and an associate can't agree on a rating, the leader makes the final call and supports it with the data. However, in the system we are describing, associates summarize their own performance and propose their own ratings. Final ratings are most often determined by mutual agreement. This doesn't mean that leaders are continually talking associates out of inflated ratings. Experience has shown that many times people hold themselves to a higher standard than their leaders do.

Because associates—not leaders—draft the reviews, they are in the best position to lead the discussions. Afterward, associates write final copies and obtain their leader's signature.

Rating Performance

It is important not to get hung up on rating scales. Yes, we do have a strongly held belief about when to use each particular scale (and will discuss this momentarily), but the scale is less important than what you are measuring and the intentions expressed when communicating about them. If you'll recall from Chapter 1, a great many organizations spend a great deal of time and money appraising associates on things that have nothing to do with strategic objectives. We don't want you to confuse the map with the territory.

For rating objectives, we recommend a three-point scale. Descriptions work better than numbers to avoid the issue of "average" connotations that we addressed earlier. A scale such as Exceeds Expectations, Meets Expectations, and Does Not Meet Expectations (or Below Expectations) works in most cases. It must be emphasized that "Meets Expectations" is a good rating; it does not denote average performance. Some organizations that have experienced years of rating inflation will struggle to accept this, but once such a new rating scale is introduced, a strong communication plan will help. Some organizations we've worked with use a five-point scale, with Far Exceeds Expectations and Far Below Expectations at the top and bottom ends, respectively. We believe rating scales should not be any more complex than that. Too often, organizations build in so much complexity that the rating—rather than the associate's performance and accomplishments—unduly commands the focus. Some consultants advocate behaviorally anchored rating scales (so far, however, we've seen no research showing that they make any difference), complicated weighting systems, or formulas that attempt to distill performance into a precise number. We feel all of these are not as useful as the time they take to develop.

In rating competencies, we recommend a three-point scale of More Than Acceptable, Acceptable, or Below Acceptable. What's being described here is this: Did the associate demonstrate or exhibit enough (or more or less than enough) of the competency during the performance cycle? The key issue in rating competencies is ensuring that the associate and the manager use specific behavioral examples (STARS, as we have mentioned before) to support the ratings. Our experience in rating performance in assessment centers, client organizations, and our own company over the past 35 years is that people behave consistently over time. For example, if you have three to five STARs that describe a person's comprehensive and accurate analysis of data, the person is most likely very high in the Analysis competency; thus, a More Than Acceptable rating is appropriate. Or, if you have three to five STARs that describe how an associate failed to take initiative when an opportunity presented itself, you most likely have someone who rates Below Acceptable in Initiative.

Obviously, this discussion simplifies the rating process somewhat. The key for organizations is that, in order to ensure some level of consistency across the organization, people must be trained in the rating scales and trained to recognize the acceptable levels of demonstrating competencies.

Many organizations use an overall rating to describe performance and link it into their pay systems. Our latest DDI research study on performance management (Bernthal, Rogers, & Smith, 2003) shows that 76 percent of the organizations surveyed use an overall rating, which we believe to be counterproductive to the main purpose of a performance management system, which is to drive performance to achieve desired results. (See Linking Compensation and Performance Management in Chapter 8. Also, see the Merck case study in Chapter 9.)

How It All Comes Together on the Forms

Following is a highly condensed version of what the completed performance worksheet might look like. An uncondensed version would probably run 3–4 pages plus the development plan.

Figure A.6: Sample Completed Performance Worksheet—Whats and Hows

Key Result Areas	Objectives	Tracking Sources	Actual Results	Ratings
Customer Satisfaction	• Achieve an average call quota of 70 calls per day.	• Statistical reports	• Averaged 71 calls a day.	Meets Expectations
	• Respond to all customer requests within 24 hours.	• Problem tracking sheets	• 3–4 calls a month weren't addressed within 24 hours.	Below Expectations
	• Receive an average minimum rating of 3 on a 5-point scale in each quarterly customer satisfaction audit.	• Audit results	• Averaged 4.2.	Exceeds Expectations

Competencies	Key Actions	Tracking Sources	Actual Results (STARs)	Ratings
Customer Focus	• Follows up with customers. • Takes responsibility for handling specific customer problems or requests.	Customer comments, self-report, leader and team feedback	Situation #2: Ned Phillips, from Cravert Industries, called to complain about being rushed off the phone before his problem was resolved. Action: I called him to apologize and then resolved his problem promptly. Result: An unhappy customer was satisfied.	Acceptable

Realizing the Benefits

Does it seem too simple? Performance management systems are not inherently mysterious. It's just that given the dearth of effective systems, it seems as though there must be a "black box" in which mysterious forces are at work. Remember, it's not about the form, although this is a good form. It's about getting everyone on the same page. It's about alignment and focus. And remember. it's about execution.

References

Armstrong, M. (2000). *Performance management: Key strategies and practical guidelines.* London: Kogan Page Ltd.

Armstrong, M. (2001). *Strategic human resource management: A guide to action.* London: Kogan Page Ltd.

Banham, R. (2003, November). Seeing the big picture. *Chief Executive* (193), 46–49.

Bernthal, P.R., Rogers, R.W., & Smith, A.B. (2003, April). *Managing performance: Building accountability for organizational success.* (HR Benchmarking Group report, Volume 4, Issue 2). Pittsburgh, PA: Development Dimensions International.

Bernthal, P.R., Sumlin, R., Davis, P., & Rogers, R.W. (1997, October). *Performance management practices survey report* (HR Benchmarking Group report, Volume 1, Issue 2). Pittsburgh, PA: Development Dimensions International.

Bernthal, P.R., & Wellins, R.S. (2001, February). *Retaining talent: A benchmarking study* (HR Benchmarking Group report, Volume 3, Issue 2). Pittsburgh, PA: Development Dimensions International.

Bossidy, L., & Charan, R. (2002). *Execution: The discipline of getting things done.* New York: Crown Business.

Byham, W.C. (2003, June). *Why managers don't change their behavior after feedback from 360° surveys and assessment centers: What you can do about it.* Presented at the annual conference of the Society for Human Resource Management, Orlando, FL.

Chambers, E.G., Foulon, M., Handfield-Jones, H., Hankin, S.M., & Michaels, E.G., III. (1998). The war for talent. *The McKinsey Quarterly, 3,* 44–57.

Charan, R., & Colvin, G. (1999, June 21). Why CEOs fail. *Fortune, 139*(12), 69–78.

Collins, J. (2001). *Good to great: Why some companies make the leap . . . and others don't.* New York: HarperCollins.

Collins, J.C., & Porras, J.I. (1994). *Built to last: Successful habits of visionary companies.* New York: HarperBusiness.

Corporate Leadership Council. (2002). *Building the high-performance workforce: A quantitative analysis of the effectiveness of performance management strategies.* Washington, DC: Author

Davis, P., Leoni, Q., & Sumlin, R. (1997). *Corporate self-defense: The legal aspects of performance management systems* [Article]. Pittsburgh, PA: Development Dimensions International.

Davis, P., & Rogers, R.W. (1997). *Pay and performance management: Making the relationship work* [Article]. Pittsburgh, PA: Development Dimensions International.

Davis, P., & Rogers, R.W. (2002). *Getting the most from your performance management system* [White paper]. Pittsburgh, PA: Development Dimensions International.

Davis, P., & Rogers, R.W. (2002). *Managing the "C" performer: An alternative to forced ranking* [White paper]. Pittsburgh, PA: Development Dimensions International.

Development Dimensions International. (2001). Research results [at BASF]. Pittsburgh, PA: Author.

Development Dimensions International. (1999). *Executing business strategy* [Leadership development course]. Pittsburgh, PA: Author.

de Waal, A.A. (2001). *Power of performance management: How leading companies create sustained value.* New York: John Wiley & Sons.

de Waal, A.A. (2002). *Quest for balance: The human element in performance management systems.* New York: John Wiley & Sons.

Dotlich, D.L., & Cairo, P.C. (2003). *Why CEOs fail: The 11 behaviors that can derail your climb to the top —and how to manage them.* San Francisco: Jossey-Bass.

Dutton, G. (2001, April). Making reviews more efficient and fair [Performance-appraisal software]. *Workforce, 80*(4), 76–81.

Evans, V., & de la Cruz-North, X. (2002). *FranklinCovey xQ™ survey results.* Salt Lake City, UT: FranklinCovey.

Fandray, D. (2001, April). The new thinking in performance appraisals. *Workforce, 80*(4), 37–40.

Flynn, P. (2001, March/April). You are simply average. *Across the Board,* 51–55.

The Gallup Organization. (2002, September 26). The four disciplines of sustainable growth: The critical elements of a performance management system. *Gallup Management Journal.* Retrieved from: http://gmj.gallup.com/content/default.asp?ci=442

Geber, B. (1988, June). The hidden agenda of performance appraisals. *Training,* 42–47.

Grote, D. (2000, May). Secrets of performance appraisal: Best practices from the masters. *Across the Board,* 14–20.

Grote, D. (2002). *The performance appraisal question and answer book: A survival guide for managers.* New York: AMACOM.

Haralson, D., & Tian, Q. (2003, September 10). Views differ on performance reviews. *USA Today,* p. B.01.

Holsinger, L., & O'Neill, C. (2002). *Effective performance management practices.* New York: Mercer Human Resources Consulting.

Holstein, W.J. (2003, November). One company, two CEOs. *Chief Executive, 193,* 30–35.

Kaplan, R.S., & Norton, D.P. (1996). *The balanced scorecard: Translating strategy into action.* Boston: Harvard Business School Press.

Kiger, P.J. (2002, May). How performance management reversed NCCI's fortunes. *Workforce, 81*(5), 48–51.

Kotter, J.P., & Heskett, J.L. (1992). *Corporate culture and performance.* New York: Free Press.

Levinson, H. (2003, January). Management by whose objectives? *Motivating People/Best of Harvard Business Review,* 107–116.

Mailliard, K. (1997, June). Linking performance to the bottom line. *HRFocus,* 17–18.

Marentette, D. (2000, December). Performance management systems: A vital key to retention. In Society for Human Resource Management & Personnel Decisions International, *SHRM performance management survey* (pp. 26–34). Alexandria, VA: Society for Human Resource Management.

Mohrman, A.M., Jr. (1989, June). *Deming versus performance appraisal: Is there a resolution?* Los Angeles: Center for Effective Organizations, School of Business Administration, University of Southern California.

Moravec, M. (1996, February). Bringing performance management out of the Stone Age. *Management Review, 85*(2), 38–42.

Neary, D.B. (2002, Winter). Creating a company-wide, on-line, performance management system: A case study at TRW, Inc. *Human Resource Management, 41*(4), 491–498.

Osterman, R. (2003, September 7). Is it really fair to grade workers on a curve? *Chicago Tribune* (final), 5.

Pardue, H.M. (2000, December). Performance appraisal as an employee development tool. In Society for Human Resource Management & Personnel Decisions International, *SHRM performance management survey* (pp. 35–43). Alexandria, VA: Society for Human Resource Management.

Park, A., with Burrows, P. (2003, November 3). What you don't know about Dell. *Business Week,* 76–84.

Rogers, R.W. (1994). *The perfect performance management system . . . well, almost!* [Article]. Pittsburgh, PA: Development Dimensions International.

Rogers, R.W., Hayden, J.W., Ferketish, J.B., & Matzen, R. (1997). *Organizational change that works: How to merge culture and business strategies for maximum results.* Pittsburgh, PA: DDI Press.

Rogers, R.W., & Smith, A.B. (2003). *Finding future perfect senior leaders: Spotting executive potential* [Article]. Pittsburgh, PA: Development Dimensions International.

Rogers, R.W., Wellins, R.S., & Conner, D.R. (2002). *The power of realization: Building competitive advantage by maximizing human resource initiatives* [White paper]. Pittsburgh, PA: Development Dimensions International.

Ryan, C. (2001, September). *Rethinking performance management Andersen performance management survey results* [Article]. Chicago: Andersen.

Saunier, A., & Mavis, M. (1998, March). Fixing a broken system. *HRFocus,* 1–4.

Schmidt, F.L., & Hunter, J.E. (1983). Individual differences in productivity: An empirical test of estimates derived from studies of selection procedure utility *Journal of Applied Psychology, 68*(3), 407–414.

Society for Human Resource Management & Personnel Decisions International. (2000, December). *SHRM performance management survey.* Alexandria, VA: Society for Human Resource Management.

Sprenkle, L.D. (1995, September). Forced ranking: A good thing for business? *Workforce, 72*(9). Retrieved from: http://www.workforce.com/section/09/feature/23/09/95/index.html

Williams, M.J. (February, 1997). Performance appraisal is dead. Long live performance management! *Harvard Management Update, 2*(2), 1–4.

About Development Dimensions International

For more than 35 years, Development Dimensions International (DDI) has helped many of the world's leading organizations hire, develop, and retain their best people by specializing in:

- Building competency-based selection systems that identify people with the right experience, skills, knowledge, and motivations for success in the job and organization.

- Developing leaders through a proven, competency-based curriculum of more than 40 courses. These courses, available in multiple languages, multiple delivery modalities, and multiple leadership areas, include Interaction Management®, the world's premier leadership development system.

- Optimizing executive talent through competency-based succession management systems, customized strategic learning experiences, and performance management systems that drive (business and culture) strategy execution.

- Building and installing performance management systems that link an organization's business strategies to clear accountabilities and that develop leaders' ability to better manage associates' performance.

DDI has worked with more than 10,000 organizations around the world and with clients from every industry as well as numerous state and federal agencies. Our organization operates 75 offices in 26 countries, offering programs in more than 10 languages.

In the past 30 years, DDI has implemented more than 300 performance management systems in client organizations. In addition, DDI's Center for Applied Behavioral Research (CABER) benchmarks performance management best practices and trends every five years. This research is conducted with a benchmark group of clients from all over the world. Combined with DDI's consulting experience, this research provides DDI with a unique perspective on the performance management field.

Loyalty is a hallmark of DDI's client base, which includes some of the most recognized names in the business world. DDI retains 95 percent of its clients year after year, and 98 percent say they would recommend DDI to others. At DDI the focus is on producing measurable, sustainable results for each client, no matter whether those results entail better customer service, reduced turnover, improved productivity, or bottom-line ROI. DDI has conducted more than 100 studies to confirm that our products and services do, indeed, produce the desired results.

For more information about programs and services available from DDI, visit our web site at www.ddiworld.com or call us between 7:30 a.m. and 5:30 p.m. (Eastern Standard Time) at 1-800-933-4463 in the United States or 1-800-668-7971 in Canada.

We welcome your comments on *Realizing the Promise of Performance Management*. Please feel free to write us at Development Dimensions International, 1225 Washington Pike, Bridgeville, PA 15017, or e-mail us at bob.rogers@ddiworld.com.

Acknowledgments

There are a host of people I would like to thank for their help in producing this book. As always in DDI, the quality of the people and their support in this project was amazing. Special recognition and thanks must go to Bill Proudfoot, Susan Conboy, and Dan Cohen:

- Bill Proudfoot was the chief editor for this book, and his contributions were invaluable. Bill's editing as well as feedback on multiple drafts provided significant improvements in numerous areas. Bill's thoroughness and skill in his profession are unmatched in my career. I can't thank him enough.

- Susan Conboy, my special assistant, has been with me for 15 years. Her patience, persistence, work ethic, and diligence in helping me put together this book have undeniably been a major part in this endeavor. From assembling the first drafts, to researching articles, to getting companies' permissions for usage, to keeping me on a schedule to get the book finished, Susan is just what one needs from an assistant. From the gentle nudges, to blocking hours of time, to honest, open feedback, Susan is a driver who made things happen even when I wanted to do something else. Susan does so many things for DDI and me that contribute to our success. I always believed no one was irreplaceable; Susan has changed my mind.

- Dan Cohen was a major contributor by helping put our first draft together. Dan's creativity and flair in writing helped set the tone and style for this book. I am forever grateful for his efforts.

There were many other people in DDI who helped in this effort by providing guidance, suggestions, and feedback with each draft. For that, my deepest appreciation goes to Linda Bisnette, Alison Bourne, Bill Coon, Patty Davis, Linda Miller, Sheryl Riddle, Audrey Smith, and David Tessmann-Keys.

The technical production of this book—from researching sources, to proofreading, to designing the graphics, to typesetting, to printing at DDI Press—has been a team effort. Many thanks to the following DDI associates and teams: Carla Fogle, Emily Ford, Shawn Garry, Jennifer Lukondi, Tammy Pordash, Lisa Weyandt, the Bindery team, the Inventory team, the Prepress team, the Press team, and the Shipping team.

The case studies in the book came from many DDI client partners who provided the information and details of their performance management implementations. I greatly appreciate their time, effort, and contributions. Thanks to Beth Braden, Federal Reserve Bank of Kansas; Stewart Davies, BT Exact; George Elsey, Sensis; Elisabeth Fleuriot, Kellogg France; Sue Forrester, Queensland Treasury; Terry Geraghty, McKesson; Karen Hanlon, Seagate; Dr. Michael Hopp, Lockheed Martin; Dr. Shirley Ross, Merck; Paul Rutledge, HCA; Lynn Summers; and Chris Toomey, Cognis.

And special thanks has to go to my boss—the chairman, CEO, and founder of DDI, Bill Byham. Bill asked me to write this book based on my years of experience consulting in the performance management area as well as my championship of DDI's in-house performance management systems for the last 20 years. In fact, he made it an objective in my annual performance plan. Bill has always been a motivating force for me in my 27 years at DDI. His encouragement, guidance, feedback, and support with this book were there just as he has been there for me in every area of my career at DDI. I can't thank him enough.

About the Author

Robert W. Rogers, president of Development Dimensions International, has long been an articulate advocate of performance management as an effective tool to drive strategic organizational change.

An acknowledged expert in effecting organizational change, he used DDI's performance management system as a primary tool to lead the company through a transformation in the 1990s that shifted its strategic focus from products and sales to customer and associate retention. He succeeded in aligning the new strategic focus with a culture that emphasizes customer focus, teamwork, innovation, and high involvement.

In 1997 he co-authored *Organizational Change That Works: How to Merge Culture and Business Strategies for Maximum Results,* a book that details the change blueprint he followed in transforming the DDI culture and in helping DDI client organizations drive change.

Before being promoted to chief operating officer in 1990, Rogers worked from 1983 to 1989 as senior vice president of DDI's regional operations. Under his leadership since then, the organization has grown steadily—from a company that grossed $7 million annually to one that currently grosses more than $110 million.

Rogers' expertise also extends into the assessment realm. Upon joining DDI in 1977 as director of DDI's Washington, D.C., office, he became heavily involved in executive assessment and performance management projects for the Federal Trade Commission, the Department of Housing and Urban Development, the Department of Health and Human Services (formerly the Department of Health, Education, and Welfare), the Department of Education, the Department of Agriculture, the National Credit Union, and many others.

One of Rogers' most significant projects was for the U.S. Equal Employment Opportunity Commission (EEOC). Following the Office of Personnel Management's uniform guidelines and procedures, he helped to design a comprehensive program for selecting regional directors for the EEOC's major field offices. He directed the assessment of more than 100 candidates and trained top-level executives in evaluating candidates' experiences and accomplishments based on specific, job-related criteria.

Rogers has delivered keynote addresses at major conferences around the world. He also continues to consult actively with senior executives in client organizations in the areas of performance management, organizational change, and leadership development. Some of these organizations include General Motors, BMW, Toyota, Pfizer, Boehringer Ingelheim, Warner-Lambert,

Gillette, Nestlé, Cadbury Schweppes, ICI Group, Citigroup, Georgia-Pacific, Transocean, and the United States Army and Air Force.

Other Written Works by Robert W. Rogers

In addition to *Organizational Change That Works,* Rogers has authored or co-authored numerous articles, monographs, and book chapters, including:

- **"Finding Future Perfect Senior Leaders: Spotting Executive Potential,"** a 2003 article that explains how companies can identify the next generation of senior leaders.

- **"The Power of Realization: Building Competitive Advantage by Maximizing Human Resource Initiatives,"** a 2002 white paper that describes the concept of realization as it relates to the success of HR initiatives.

- **"The Psychological Contract of Trust,"** a 2003 monograph that addresses the need to build trust with employees and how to build trust in today's turbulent business environment.

- **"Creating a High-Involvement Culture Through a Value-Driven Change Process,"** a 1997 monograph about how organizations can transform themselves to drive business results by establishing a foundation of values that supports a new company direction.

- **"How to Hire a First-Rate Sales Force,"** a 1989 article about the process of improving the quality of sales force hires based on proper selection criteria and proven methods to obtain accurate data for applicants.

- **"Diagnosing Organization Cultures for Realignment,"** a chapter from the 1994 book *Diagnosis for Organizational Change* by Ann Howard and associates.

Other Books from DDI

Empowered Teams: Creating Self-Directed Work Groups That Improve Quality, Productivity, and Participation by Richard S. Wellins, William C. Byham, and Jeanne M. Wilson

HeroZ™—Empower Yourself, Your Coworkers, Your Company by William C. Byham with Jeff Cox (available in English, French, German, Spanish, Korean, Chinese, Arabic, and Portuguese)

Inside Teams: How 20 World-Class Organizations Are Winning Through Teamwork by Richard S. Wellins, William C. Byham, and George R. Dixon

Landing the Job You Want: How to Have the Best Job Interview of Your Life by William C. Byham with Debra Pickett

Organizational Change That Works: How to Merge Culture and Business Strategies for Maximum Results by Robert W. Rogers, John W. Hayden, and B. Jean Ferketish, with Robert Matzen

The Selection Solution: Solving the Mystery of Matching People to Jobs by William C. Byham with Steven M. Krauzer

The Service Leaders Club by William C. Byham with Ray Crew and James H.S. Davis

Shogun Management™: How North Americans Can Thrive in Japanese Companies by William C. Byham with George Dixon

Succeeding With Teams: 101 Tips That Really Work by Richard S. Wellins, Dick Schaaf, and Kathy Harper Shomo

Team Leader's Survival Guide by Jeanne M. Wilson and Jill A. George

Team Member's Survival Guide by Jill A. George and Jeanne M. Wilson

Zapp!® in Education by William C. Byham with Jeff Cox and Kathy Harper Shomo

Zapp!® Empowerment in Health Care by William C. Byham with Jeff Cox and Greg Nelson

Zapp!® The Lightning of Empowerment—revised edition by William C. Byham with Jeff Cox (original edition available in English, French, German, Japanese, Dutch, Chinese, Korean, Portuguese, and Spanish)

Zapp!® The Lightning of Empowerment—the video

INDEX

Realizing the Promise of
Performance Management

strategic priorities, 66; driving accountability, 66; execution of, 16; at HCA, 50; Larry Bossidy and, 3; supporting cultural strategy, 28, 30, 33

CARE survey, 32–33

cascading accountability, 19, 65, 67

case studies, BASF, 98–100; BT Exact, 117–118; Cognis, 37–38; Federal Reserve Bank of Kansas City, 36–37; Getting the Bugs Out, 59; HCA, Inc. (MidAmerica Division), 49–51; Kellogg Company, France, 21–23; Lockheed Martin, 127–129; McKesson Information Solutions, 23–25; Merck, 114–117; Queensland Treasury Corporation, 83–84; Seagate Technology, 78–82; Sensis, 60–62

champions, 10, 20

coach, 58; defined, 57; leader's role as, 45

coachable moments, 58

coaching, 10–11, 55–57, 70–72, 93, 95, 110, 125–126, 141, 150; to achieve or exceed expectations, 5; and bill of rights, 73; as corporate self-defense, 122; evaluating system effectiveness, 76; at HCA, 50; importance of training, 12, 56, 70; at Kellogg France, 22; at Merck, 115

Cognis, 37–38

Collins, James, 28, 69

communication, 54, 71, 86, 132; advantages of, 45; at Boldcase, 138; as a competency, 97–98; Deming-level, 56; as a driver of improved performance, 8; as effective strategy, 30; at Enron, 35; of expectations, 58; generating open, 45; at HCA, 50–51; infrequent, 12; linking compensation and performance management, 100; ongoing, 56–57; quality of, 11; and realization, 109; at Seagate, 82; and trust, 47; value of, 58

compensation, analysis at Merck, 116; appraisals serve as crutches for decisions, 86; basics, 103; at HCA, 50; Johnson & Johnson Credo, 29; link to performance management, 74, 86, 100; one of two most difficult HR systems, 134; quality of, 47; at Queensland Treasury Corporation, 83; when combined with effective performance management, 95; why people leave, 44

competencies (dimensions), 17, 19, 47–48, 55, 93, 112, 119, 121; at BASF, 99; in bill of rights, 73; at Boldcase, 137; at Cognis, 38; defined, 19, 147; hows of performance, 147; at McKesson, 24; with multirater instruments, 96; as a point of integration for HR systems, 113; rating, 154–155; at Seagate, 79; using to fill open positions, 74–75

consultants; benefits of using, 131; how to select, 134; references, 135; role of, 132

leader/associate relationships, 44; quality of the compensation package, 47; realizing an engaged workforce, 48; training managers and associates, 70; what people want from work, 42; why people leave, 44; winning the war for talent, 42

Maximizing Alignment and Performance (MAP), 79–81

McKesson Information Solutions, 23–25, 76, 164

McKinsey & Co., 41

McNerney, W. James, Jr., 90

measurement, 75–76; accountability, 67; an interesting phenomenon, 68; lack of, 11; at Merck, 115–116; methods of, 17–18; techniques, 114; tracking progress, 145

Mercer Management Consulting, 12

Merck, 76, 114–117, 164

multirater feedback, 95

multirater instruments, 95; accuracy of, 96; inflated ratings on, 96; questions to ask about, 96

multirater results, when to use, 95

multirater surveys, 95; at BASF, 98–99; at Lockheed Martin, 128; at Merck, 115

Nasser, Jacques, 91

Nordstrom's, 30

objectives, defined, 144; how many, 147; SMART, 145

organizational change, 18, 85; at BASF, 98

Organizational Change that Works, 27

organizational culture, 27; building through forced ranking, 90

organizational values, 6, 27–28, 30–33, 66, 101, 105; at Lockheed Martin, 127

performance appraisal, 5, 55, 71, 85, 120, 124; as a crutch for compensation decisions, 86, 101; Deming and, 53–55; focus on what or how, not both, 87; minimize involvement, 86; traps of, 85–87; versus performance management, 5–7; why people leave, 44

performance management, align to support business goals and drive results, 66; balance whats and hows, 69; best practices, 66–77; cascade accountabilities, 67; and consultants, 131–133; and cultural strategy, 33; and Deming, 53–55; evaluate regularly, 75; the failures of, 10–13; implementing as a five-step process, 109; legal aspects of, 120–121; line management drives system, 77; link to other systems, 73;

at Cognis, 37; cultural strategy, 27; performance management as a tool for, 19–20, 123; the process for, 18; proportionate to alignment, 16–17; six steps for, 19; and technology, 123; versus strategy development, 15

summary statement, defined, 102

Summers, Lynn, 164

technology, 42; at Lockheed Martin, 127–129; no substitute for human interactions, 126; and training, 127; what to expect from, 124–126

Tuomey, Chris, 164

tracking progress, 145

traps (of performance appraisal processes), 85–87

U.S. Marine Corps, 27

values, organizational, 6, 17, 28, 30–34, 46, 48, 66, 85, 101, 104, 120, 141, 147; at BASF, 99; at BT Exact, 117; at DDI, 32–33; at GE, 33; at Kellogg France, 21–23; living the, 30; at Lockheed Martin, 127; at Seagate, 79

vision, organizational, 15, 66, 85, 111, 140; at BASF, 99; at Merck, 114

Watson Wyatt Worldwide, 4

Welch, Jack, 12, 33; on living GE's values, 33; supporter of forced ranking, 90; value of open, honest feedback, 92

whats, 65–66, 140, 144, 150; aligned with cultural strategies, 17; balance with hows, 65–66, 69; defined, 17; at Kellogg France, 22

"Why CEOs Fail," 15